Praise for Like a Vermeer & Other Poems

Like a Vermeer gives us a passionate poet, his chants echoing through the palaces of Rumi, Rimbaud, and Marvin Gaye. Yousuf Zaigham's "brazen words with mascara-flecked eyes" come pouring out like flowers, like electricity, like a whirling holy dance of language. He offers both praise and complaint to God-"God of blue iguanas, purple herons, and strawberry-margarita havens"-to other poets, to his parents, to his lovers, and to himself. This is a river of a book, its currents richly colored, its rhythms always pushing on, its surfaces shining and its depths profound."

—Robert King, Director, Colorado Poets Center & author of *What It Was Like*.

Yousuf Zaigham's glistening lines roll across the page in wave after wave like a mesmerizing surf. Each line, almost complete in itself, baths both heart and mind in the salt spray of "*pomegranate raptures*" with "*guava-sweet melancholy.*" I love the wisdom in these poems. Full-spectrumed, they reflect beauty, passion, ecstasy and reason as they roll in at you with roaring exuberance. It becomes evident that Zaigham's poetic heritage in part came from Rumi, Rimbaud & Rilke. I return to Zaigham's ocean again and again to hear his singing lines break against my mind and heart to reshape my shore once more.

—P.D. Strobridge, author of *Unmasking The Heart*

In lush mastery of his second language, Yousuf Zaigham writes, "…I have given you stunning jewels." Indeed, as you read this extraordinary volume of poetry, reminiscent of Rumi and Hafiz, you will imagine the poet as a master jeweler. Zaigham's gift for opulent language and mystical imagery reveals "bloodstones and carnelian luster", "diamond-cut handsomeness", "blue pearls", even a "16-carat swoon". Like perfect gemstones, his poems entice with facets, shadings, luster—all beauty and brilliant fire.

—Andrea L. Watson, *Braided Lives: A Collaboration Between Artists and Poets*

In "Like a Vermeer" we listen in on a wide-ranging and somewhat friendly quarrel with life and with a God who gives and also takes away. As we read we meet a poet who's in love with life, with colors, and with words. He's caught in an internal quarrel between gratitude and protest, and though he asks, "Why me, especially?" the reader senses that this disjunct is a necessary part of the poet's life and indeed, has become his pleasure.

—Lois Bebe Hayna, Author of *Standing Still*

LIKE A VERMEER & OTHER POEMS

LIKE A VERMEER & OTHER POEMS

Yousuf Zaigham

iUniverse, Inc.
New York Lincoln Shanghai

Like a Vermeer & Other Poems

iUniverse books may be ordered through booksellers or by contacting:

iUniverse
2021 Pine Lake Road, Suite 100
Lincoln, NE 68512
www.iuniverse.com
1-800-Authors (1-800-288-4677)

ISBN-13: 978-0-595-40974-7 (pbk)
ISBN-13: 978-0-595-85330-4 (ebk)
ISBN-10: 0-595-40974-1 (pbk)
ISBN-10: 0-595-85330-7 (ebk)

Printed in the United States of America

Contents

Acknowledgement

A special thanks to Andrea Watson, my patient editor, for her unflagging support.

ALL I HAVE DONE IS THIS

Readers/voyeurs,

I have taken your hydra dreads,
the grenadine suns in your tequila sunsets,

your three-penny tremors & frets,
the menagerie of your Scarlett
O'Hara shames, betrayals, upsets,
the whispering magentas of your heart-stopping
rhinestone flecked thongs,

your secret longings for the "shilling whores"
in fleshpots of Bangkok & Hanoi,
the chalcedony of your jealous streaks,
the sap & incense of your rare pomegranate
raptures with my wild embellishments,

the bruised mints of your Job-like agons
& quarrels with Elohim, Lucifer & the tax inspector,
the greasy spills of your TV séances,
the flying shrapnels of your tense
sniper-alley marriages & alliances,

your ritual shuffles like rain dances
at the whooping ballparks,
your Sangria swaggers in cheeky honkytonks
with sad-eyed waitresses & Tammy Wynette
wailing on hoarse jukeboxes.

I floated all that with the summer blaze
of yellow barberries & scarlet flaxes
& wrapped the concoction in the migrant trills
of blue jays & crimson-breasted barbets

& shook it well with Apollo's insolence
& garnished it with the beads & florets
of my guava-sweet melancholy
& wholesaled it as *my* peacock poetry.

PALACE OF RUMI

When you display that rosy cheek,
you set the stones
a-spinning for joy.
Once again put forth your head from the veil,
for the sake of dumbstruck
lovers, that learning may lose the way,
that the man of reason may break
his science to pieces;
So long as you are desirous,
know that this desire of yours
is an idol; when you have become beloved,
after that there is no existence for the desirous.
 —Jalaluddin Rumi *Mystical Poems of Rumi 1*

You ask me why I dare stick out my neck,
Bull-headed, why my heart's so full of rage?
It is because I come from Antaeus's lineage—
God hurls his darts at me, I throw them back.
I am inspired by the Vengeful God
Who planted his angry kiss upon my brow.
   —Nerval *Les Chimerès*

THE GOOD DELUGE

How many mind-hurtling bolts of books,
God Almighty,
you will send to this gaunt tree of mine,
to flood my already pummeled senses,
to notch up the levees of my yearnings,
to sting my hungers, to stoke my madness,
to make me squirm like a newborn infant
groping again & again for the first mouthful
of a nipple-blossom.

These books are like the hundred
promenading beauties on moon-soaked
Chowpatty beach in Mumbai,
whose litchi tongues I will never savor
or paint with my raptures,
whose sweet-limbed coconut flesh
will never lollop against
my nuanced knees or chest,
whose moon-temples
will float on alien islands
like the shoals of tulips
in Amsterdam gardens,
blooming heedless to my famished eyes.

How many more books,
God of Marx & Montaigne,
sculptor of Vikrum Seth & Rushdie,
kiln-keeper of Pindar & Proust,
to shame my prying, to taunt my guilt
of never knowing the countless
minnowing stars sparkling
in the lake of knowledge
& knowing full well that Africa, India
& China are still rustling
in a lagoon of slumber
& over-pregnant with a billion wonders!

DON'T ASK!

All things are but masks at God's beck and call,
They are symbols that instruct us that God is all.
                          —Farid Ud-Din Attar

You are the splitter of Dawn, the Lord of the day break,
you open hundred doors and say, Come in!
                                    —Rumi

If prophets wouldn't have come, the splendid mornings
would have been enough to be God's evidence.
                                    —Josh

You the great homesickness that we could
never shake off.
                          —Rilke

Whose tangy succulence sleeps like nectar
in the burrows of jackfruits & pineapples?

Whose blazing stare never leaves us alone
in the cardinal sage raptures of dusks & daybreaks?

Who plunges us in this great homesickness
that we can never break off with liqueur & quietus?

Whose many cadences I have heard so often
in the tidal chords of my cocktail blood?

Whose steady hand steadies sun's bubbly
cinnabar strobe on Grand Canyon's rims?

Whose carnivorous yen
lures the insects in a Venus trap
to their larkspur perdition?

Whose spearing glance stuns
a gliding pelican on an Easter break?

Whose brazen blood swells in the shoots
& cells of vanda's butterfly wings & raptures?

Whose fingers strum red maples' flaming harps
& ignite the brass section of marigolds?

Whose adularia eyes spy on us
through the veils of black-eyed Susan?

Whose lilac philandering made my wife
twice pregnant & plump?

Whose vintage cabernet keeps the planets dance
in an endless tarantella?

Whose rumba throbs in the sweet vertigo
of the fire flies, damsel fishes & razorbills?

Yet, Darwin was no farther from today's verities.

No Annabel,

there is no spook, no phantom gardener
snooping behind
the flowering henna & may apples
tending the meadows & dells,
no blades of blue grass
sing of the lonely lyricist.

No tiptoeing painter slinks
behind the sepia glades or purple bluffs
to make Turner & Gainsborough green with envy.

Picasso like—an incubus of galactic proportions
Nature cannot control its ever-forging fingers.
It keeps re-inventing itself,
impervious & purblind to all written scripts,
librettos & subtexts, this Mother of all fables,
witchcrafts, incantations, gnome trees
& goose bumps just made it all up as it went over
the eonian grids & millenniums' musical scales.

PERHAPS WE WERE NOT MADE FOR EACH OTHER

God, you & I were, perhaps,
not made for each other.

You never grew under my soft
red-brown digitalis skin.

We haven't spoken much since my awkward teens
when I discovered masturbation & D.H. Lawrence
& noticed that so many dazzling men & women
had escaped your internment camps
& were not any more miserable or sullen or at risk
than your devout, bloodthirsty orderlies
who raved daily from gilded pulpits.

Now I am quite content with this no star-spangled,
humdrum no-frills life you granted me
& I have never complained.

I am now at peace with my quotidian lot
& look forward to my lento shipwreck.

I have no stomach or spleen left
to argue whether we were rolled off
from Adam's ribs or a dove's horn
or were spat out by a snake god
or are descended from seaweeds or a leviathan
or grew out of a giant banyan's sprawl.

I suspect there is no time left
to mend our differences.

I have no wish to figure out
where I get mapped out in yours
or Marx's astrological plots & sub-texts.

What will now be the point of a rapprochement?

We have lived for so long
in separate galaxies & constellations,
but my children are another matter.

Who knows, you & they
may just get along splendidly.

I was always skittish of any fealty
that suspended
or rudely banished my reason
or benumbed my logical antlers & sensors.

God, You always sounded too overbearing,
always frothing with hubris.

You acted so much like my abrasive daddy.
I couldn't handle two imperious fathers.

May be you have changed since my teens
& are no longer a diehard Stalinist
in your controlling logistics
or bullish on compliance & in
reaching instantly for the jugular
if you don't get your royal mandate.

It is too late for me to tune in to your Web site
or toddle up to your old pad in Mount Sinai,
anything more than a truce
& a warm handshake will be an encumbrance.

That is all I can tolerate,
That is all my shot nerves will take.

I wish my children well, I wish you well.

I wish the three of you could seek a new beginning
& share a new vernacular of intimacy
that you never advertised for me

& I never cared to dig in my flinty stubbornness.

THE MANDALA

God, I dreamt of you so often
that I became *your* purple primrose dream.

I never had to rush each morning,
after tedious ablution to the gilded temples
& lofty cathedrals to lasso your grace.

I just had to look inward
to catch your cattleya glimpse,
to touch the rainbow
of your kaleidoscopic face,
to fly into the hushed heavens of your rage
like the blaze of vermilion irises
because dear God, I too have become your mandala.

THE SADISM OF YAHWEH

When I asked for your hand, beloved,
all the suitable young men & eligible dreamers
in your Shiite neighborhood
wanted you to be their life-mate.

Your were a dew red zinnia,
a heart-stopping eye-pearl in lilac satin,
a thunderbolt of grace
in cinnabar sandals & purple braids.

Who knew then, my precious,
that the ocher tide would turn against us
& your plumeria face would become
an ever raging insurgency
of acne & heartbreaks

as if an avenging Yahweh with the black
heart of a cosmos blossom
was finally showing me my place
as if he was using
your embattled countenance
like a sinister voodoo doll
to torment me
everyday of the month!

PRELUDE TO AN EPIPHANY

If I were a Zen Buddhist
I would have convinced
my jealous God that I don't need
to visit his pagoda temples
to kiss the gold locks
in his loosened braids.
That all my vireo-songs
& scarlet-ringed barbet rhymes
were nothing but pleas
for his indulgence & pickings.
That the agonies of my crested flesh
for Suzy Wong or Sally Fleming
were nothing but the muffled
moans & allegro longings
for his invisible lips, his inscrutable arms,
his handsome breast of nestled lights.

That the raptures igniting my blood
when I made love to some foxy girl
were my desperate acts to lock
his unyielding glance, to crash into
his unwilling arms & when I humored
some darling face in my college days
to cause a grinning fest, I was looking
for his approving nod
like a fledgling stand-up comic,
& when I soaped & bathed a beauty's
pearl-rose bod
by a seaside cottage in Carmel
or got down on my hands & knees
to kiss her tufted spider wart triangle,
my ears were hooked and keen, my eyes
were spiked & peeled, my hydrangea heart
was in a 16-carat swoon for perchance

I might catch my Lord slaloming
through his splendid tenor sax like
John Coltrane by a blue jade bluff,
perchance I might see his Adonis grin

in the mazurka of waves,
perchance he might call
my pathetic, lecherous name
& amble towards me
in a cloudburst of
bloodstones & carnelian flare
& clutch my quivering slipshod hand
& whisper into my dizzying heart
"Listen man, I am right here
as your soul's anchor,
don't meander any longer
as that footloose, foolhardy, straggler moon
that you have resembled so often!"

CLOSENESS

You would not seek me if
you had not already found me.
                    —Pascal

Pining so ardently for your electric lily-riffs,
your acacia strains, your pulsating chords,
the glinting refrains of your alto sax,
God, I finally became your sibyl hands,
your bopping eyes, your ululating heart,
your syncopating feet!

THE SKYLARK

God, how wonderfully sly of you
that you wouldn't let me ever have
real friends or a wife who might
adore my sonnets
as she worships her bobtail cats & tulips.
You didn't give me parents or siblings
who might swear by my staggering talents.
You handed me down offsprings
who might not lose a sepal of sleep

if all my poems were burnt down in a nasty blaze
& then you had the nerve to fedex me
to a green house of a country infested with
rampant & skirling prejudice & yet
I rose like a skylark to hug your dimpled stars,
to rival your flaunted oversold concerts
& pay you back ever so graciously
for every nickel of minor gifts that you
begrudgingly dropped in my beggar's hat.

THE STIGMATA OF RADIANCE

God, how could I resist your pleasure
when you pierced my heart & assailed me
on one lackluster evening & now I am paying
dearly for that cheap kaffir lily rapture.
What heady price for the faux castanets
of immortality you have exacted from me?
What steady drain of Melatonin,
what cortisol spikes & pricey coffee beans
to keep up with your divine banalities & high jinks
& then the daily drag to turn them
into gem-studded tiaras & necklaces?
God Almighty, there is no pleasure left
in being your hanger-on & fav icon,
a quivering aperture for your stiletto lights.
God, why me specially to run off
your unbridled opulence?
Your constant buffeting has made me morose,
listless, lonesome, wan & sleep-thirsty.
I was supposed to be so pleased
by the gifts of "uncultured" pearls

that you keep dropping in my jewel-casket
but I am just about ready to slide into the shredder,
the taxing covenant between you & me
to decode twenty-four-seven your cantata snores,
your elliptical Sweet William whispers,
your Jurassic moans, your geranium jeers,
your turquoise-blue whimpers,
your colonnades of grunts, your Freudian slips,
the Grand Canyons of your abysmal silences,
your clumsy masks, veneers, veils & stratagems
into breathtaking *Turando & Aida*
& then to carry all the wretched blame
& suffer the noxious bad reviews & midnight reruns,
swallow the dubious credits that you must be dealing
while you, my impish, insensate trickster,
keep laying evermore lavish, psychedelic eggs
in my poetic nest to be hatched, to be hatched, to be hatched
till I drop dead like the cursed empress Mumtaz Mahal
for whom Shah Jehan built that doleful Taj Mahal!

A MARKED MAN

God Almighty, I heard it from the grapevines
that my lease on life is getting
closer to the finish line,
that our lovers' spats will become a bouquet
of silly scandals in cabbalistic tabloids.
Who will serve you then on his hands & knees,
your royal majesty?
Who will scrounge around
to pick up the cinder cones
for your water pipes to soothe your emphysema
or make your sobs glitter
like flaming Burmese rubies?
God, I am your signet ring
to radio-wave your dim glimmers.
I am your Sybil lips to amplify your faint murmurs.
Who will cut-glass your shrill screams
into flashy diamonds
or distill his own blood like an alchemist
to embellish the cheap muslin of your anguish?
God, whose ovens' blaze will soften
the bitterness of your arctic winters?
Who will build the slit-trenches
to rest your gouty knees
or grin profusely at your risqué jokes to cheer up
a troubled world menaced
by suicide bombers,
who will revise your clichéd verse
into vaulted fireworks?

Think of all that inventory of loss
before you order
my wife's widowhood!

THE SHOWER

This is the third week, Lord God,
that I have stayed persuaded
that life is not the Promised Land,
not the sweet ambrosia
that your marquee prophets whispered
in our juvenile hearts.

How long, Lord God, would it take you
to figure this one out
& do the proper thing
before I can prove to your chagrin
that what I was forced to take in,
as a squirming fetus,
I have every right to decline at any age
without any shame & with some assistance
by a furrowed faced man
in white tunic, gold tasseled hair
tutoring me how to turn on
the sweet shower of death
in the privacy of my living room
while all my good friends
& next of kin peer over with fondness.

JEALOUSY

We made women the apparel for men.
                              —*Quran*

God, if I give you back this much envied warm-up vest
of lipstick-mauve incandescence keenly scented
with immortality's azaleas & dispatched
by you with such nepotistic affection,
will you then guarantee that no man would
ever slip on my beloved's svelte body
or lap her cherry blossom cannoli tongue
or wade her long Nicole Kidman legs
after you shut off my breathing?

LIKE FATHER, LIKE SON

But Friends, we have come too, late! The gods are indeed alive
But above our heads, up there in another world
They are there endlessly active, & seem to heed little
Whether we are alive that is how much the heavenly ones care.
                                        —Fredrick Holderlin
We live our lives forever taking leave.
                    —Rilke

God, you planned your life "forever taking leave"

in effect ruining ours.

Your departures, it seems, far exceeded
your arrivals because of the lengths
of your generous sabbaticals
as if you made a sad habit
of running off to other swarthy islands
with lovelier sunsets & shinier rums
right after our births
& leaving our mothers bleeding with frets
& longings & stuck with trashy suitors
so now don't blame us
when we frantically abandon
our sons & daughters
just starting kindergarten.

God you shouldn't encumber us
with the draconian tablets of do's & don'ts
when you yourself can't remember
the last time you called me to celebrate
my first soccer goal, my first puppy kiss,
my first brave rising
with splintered left eyebrow
without tear-misted eyes
after being pounded & booted
by the fat school bully.

RUMI'S STAIRCASE

Rumi never browsed my verses,
lithesome & big bosomed like a lap dancer
so why should I pour the eggnog gold
& rum of my evenings
in Rumi's copper carfare?

Why should I go blowing primly
in his lucent flute to find my own voice?

Didn't I hear God's crooning in the first place
in the adagio hammering of my heart
against the thick-beaded rains?

Didn't I glean God's gleaming pseudonyms
scrawled in the graffiti of the stars?

Can't I rake by myself how the meadow-saffron sun
wades through the hyacinth lakes of the planet?

Haven't I seen the fish-clouds quaking
like a grayling's dorsal fins?

Haven't I inhaled my Leila's scent
In camellia's vermilion laced negligee?

Haven't my eyes bled with thanks
in the sweet downpour of a pewter moon?

Haven't I felt cuddled by the pendulous arms
of the sea in a dizzying pram?

Haven't I sobbed like a candle watching
the rain lily incandescence of a little girl smiling
in slow motion nibbling a Sunday cartoon?

Haven't I jolted in my groins
by the terrific blossoms of a made-up hooker
that I had spotted in Versailles's gardens?

Haven't I felt one with the organza-green sedge
while watching the scraggy skiffs gliding past
Istanbul's skylines in Bosphorus

that I am somehow caught between
the blazing dance of the minarets
embellishing the Ottoman mosques?

Haven't I caressed God's hands
a dozen times in one evening

while driving through
a bossa nova thunder storm
when I felt in my chest-cage
the wild percussions of God's tenor sax
swooping down Interstate 90?

This maddening thirst to liaise
with all the flash points of creation
is my mystical quilt.

My poems' busy murals are my hymns to God.

I am his stunning epiphany in F-sharp.

I roller-blade on the violet pimpernel
steams of my cravings
so why should I pour the cabernet of my love
in old cups of Rumi to endear God?

I don't need Rumi's staircase
to touch my Lord's gilt ankles,

my poetry is the wine barrel
gladly paid in full by a grateful God?

A LATE NIGHT VISIT

God, had you been fidgeting for long
by the whiny balustrade?

Cheating on you is the farthest thing
from my mind.

Lately, I have been much too tangled up.
My mother is visiting from Leeds

& my son's car blues are not over yet—
first a deadbeat battery & then
a scary car-break-in.

When I fetch my mother from my sister's place
she & I battle like two over-the-hill geriatric cats,
always at each other's throats & nerve endings,

savagely tearing up our papyrus metaphysics,
calling each other names, cussing together
the hour of my Immaculate Conception & birth.

But God, you already know
all these bickering minuets
so enough of these old bitch alibis.

When folks hear me whisper
they think I am mocking Prince Hamlet

or Saint Matthew in pristine wilderness
debating with himself while chomping on
anti-oxidant black berries
or protein-rich fat bugs.

God, lucky for us
that no one is around at 2 AM
& a balmy breeze from Pikes Peak
has started a lovely ballad
redolent of Billie Holiday.

God, let me steady your gnarled hands,
your lento gait wiry with arthritis,

let me set up your ivory-nubbed cane,
your guano-smudged orthopedic shoes,

your worn out leather gaiters,
your sweaty Red Wing cap
& deep orange cardigan
still fogging with acanthus clouds in that corner.

Let me make us a pot of steaming green tea
& serve it in silver-lapis Iranian demitasses.

Damn good for your squirming, old,
fibrillating partridge heart & your asthma.

If your old trifocals
are bugging your bleary eyes,
please take them off
& I will place them on the mantle.

Let me fire up your favorite indigo-fringed
Egyptian hookah,

tell me what flavored tobacco will buoy your mood.
I just have three flavors left in my pantry—
Pineapple, apricot & strawberry.

Have you already switched to Sweet-N-Low
or should I put the 3 heaping teaspoons of sugar
you usually float in your syrupy tea?

It would just take a few moments
& then let's chatter & twitter
& quibble the night away

under the stirring stars
& waft of jasmine
& over the violet sucking, hazelnut coughing,
plum gurgling & russet crackling
of the narghile water pipe.

A HOT TIP FOR GOD

God, in William Blake's painting of you,
you look smashingly debonair
like a great muscled lion-king
jumping through a blazing
orange-gold hoop letting the infant
universe sluice down
from the v womb of your two fingers
while your yarrow-white beard flaps leftward
like a brewing Caribbean hurricane

& again you are looking dapper & grand
in your wind-swept beard seemingly flirting
with a buck-naked
& a little flushed Master Adam
in Michelangelo's rendition of your shenanigans

but, dear God, times have vastly changed:
you will be better served
& will look at your arresting best
as a great God if you let
Thomas Edison model
for your creative swirl
& if you are skeptical of the scientists
& madcap inventors

then please settle for Picasso—
that thunder-fest Spaniard from Malaga
even though he is absolutely vainglorious,
superstitious, a veteran heart breaker,

frequent patron of brothels,
a terminal two-timing SOB
& often hugely cantankerous
he must surely fit the tall bill
of your never mellowing down,
never standing still
whooshing, supersonic, stupendous
exuberance quite gallantly!

LORD REMEMBER ME

Lord God, don't grieve for me when I am gone,
keep me shimmying in your
filigreed ragas & songs.
Remember how I fawningly gazed
at those hoodoos in Utah's Bryce Canyon
blazing like giant crimson temples
all joining hands in supplication
as if for your kindling eyes.

Lord, remember me as I remembered you
repeatedly in the sapphire samba
of moray eels,
in the undulating purple eyes of sea scorpions
dappled like lilies,
in the drifting rainbows of clown fishes,
in the gorgeous bones of sea urchins,
in the purple bloom of Douglas irises,
in the dusky blossoms of sea anemones,
in the morphing of rose sedums
into blazing bronze when autumns came.

Lord God, I will remember you
in the ruby-green sweetness of guavas,
in the brilliant red leaves of Bengal almonds.
in the whirlwind feast of a sunflower star.

Remember me in the arctic nights of eternity,
in the waxing & waning of the lover-moon
as I missed you in the water holes
of Vienna & Istanbul
when my longing for you would alight
my scarlet minivet heart
& you would glow in my liatrus reveries
& would seed pearls in my eyes
while a hushed cambric sky
quivered with lilac tattoos
& smeared lipstick of Cholla cactus.

The Longing

God, I know how the pink cassias
bloom just before the heavy monsoons
& the first shower slaughters all the blossoms.
God, I have no blossoms left
on my bare bone branches but still no breaking news
of your approaching torrents!

God's Nightmare

God, I thought I had completely
woken up from your nightmare
since my velveteen teens;
then what is this midnight longing
that can't be quieted even after
I have slept with a splendid woman
& all the Dicentra books of the world
lie bare by my feet & I can travel far & deep
to the Geisha land or to an odalisque's Kasbah
to fawn over my favored swamp lilies
& yet you still haunt my poetry's atrium
like a ghost-lit dream & I feel
I am again bewitched,
bothered & bewildered
like an over-sexed teenager
or is it now the closing footfalls
of death that have prompted me
to seek frantically your flighty fragrance
& your wild-indigo lullabies?

Homecoming

God, why should I kneel before your flaunted images,
your stela & your carvings done by other Masters
while I myself have become one of your dazzling
lithographs, a missal neoning your hundred names
so when the mourners will raise on their shoulders
the broken wings of my time-worn body,
they will be bringing you
the tiny ripraps of yourself—
a little embarrassing for your binging ego I admit
but it will be *our* homecoming nonetheless.

FORGIVENESS

We made man from clotted blood.
                    —*Quran*

God, even if you may hold
the haloed chalice of Florence
like a Buddhist mendicant monk
& would come to me bearing gifts
of saffron-red tulips & peacock orchids
asking for my forgiveness
for the offense of pouring your light
into my dusky knot of blood,
I am still unwilling to let
bygones be bygones
because the scandal of death
still grates so cloppingly
on my harpsichord nerves.

SERENADE

God, at age fourteen distraught with
your demurring & your inscrutable
grin of a school boy sniffing glue,
I thought I could just move on
with my cravings like a footloose waterfall
that knew its moorings.
There was so much more glitter
to summer nights, sultry as Josephine Baker,
more juice to bluegrass jams,
banjos, mandolins, strings, harmonicas,
acoustic guitars & grinding harps
than chasing your insidious scent.
That my stormy arias will
somehow drown out your ever nagging
lavender whispers & I think
I almost succeeded
but look who is back there trudging
under the window of your lapis balcony
after all these crazy years
like a stupid hillbilly
serenading for the luscious pulp
of your breeze-plucked cantatas.

JOHN DONNE'S DIVINE POEMS

I am a little peeved by John Donne's
collateral distress over our final crumbling
as if he never saw a lively baby squirrel
grow old & frail & then fade out
like a spent flame. How easy it is
to accept death the moment
we stop coddling ourselves
as half-angels & see that we are
bona fide siblings
of kangaroos, chinchilla buck rabbits
& loquacious house pigeons.

FETISH

Lord God, you made us with
so much cunning & skill
only to raze us with such
great stealth & relish
as if we were moths, snails,
slugs or centipedes.

Like a Michelangelo why do you always
find some lurking flaw in us to splinter us
& to start up investing your stunning gifts
in a new obsession or fetish
as if we have never been more than
a bunch of Barbie dolls for your wanton pleasure.

THE RADIANCE

Lord, I am not worthy that
you should enter under my roof.
—*A Pre-communion Catholic Prayer*

God you have been lolling in my heart's gorge
out-swelling me like a viridian sea—
wave upon wave, glare over glare.
When I will finally explode & flare
the world will be blinded by the bleedings
of a thousand suns. God, by the way, how did you
guess my heart had such endless suppleness?

TRANSCENDENTAL *KAMA SUTRA*

Lord God, I am dancing as fast as I can
but this verbena giddiness is killing me
but how far could I have soared
without this savage rapture?
This footloose drift of dreams,
keeps me scuttling like
the braided magma sprinting
through cinder planes
just to kiss the blue tongue of the Pacific.

It has been hard as hell trying to make love
to every blooming lettuce-coral,
swirling acacia & eucalyptus grove,
every ringed nipple, pierced navel,
pearled tongue, inebriated rain lily,
& tangoing galaxy of your restive,
brazen Isadora Duncan Creation.

INFIDELITIES

God of blue iguanas, purple herons
& strawberry-margarita havens,
forgive me my so many
magenta infidelities
flaming like dendrobium buds
so indiscreetly committed
in the bathhouses of my poetry
& in my sinning heart
for lusting after women younger
than my daughter
but I seek greater forgiveness
for the weakness of my valor
for never responding
to the occasional come-ons
& faint encouragements
from the flirtatious glances
of these foxy women
igniting the forbidden air.

GOD AS ODYSSEUS

God, I understand perfectly
that your address book is filled
with gorgeous galaxies
to hop from one
to the other's flowerbed
for your ongoing one night stands
but how does it justify abandoning
our mother-earth & poor us
to fight & ward off
ungainly suitors
filled with loaded bladders, beer-stench,
a pile of half-eaten salads
& cheeseburgers by our swimming pool
& in the lumbering living room?

THE LUMP

God, you seldom begin like a lump
in my throat but more often
as a scarlet-sage blaze in my heart
wanting me to torch
every silk curtain,
knock down every vine hedge & wall,
kick every acacia bush in your garden
& smash the showy fountain
in your courtyard because you have
a rhinestone heart & can't peer
beyond the napes
of your up close teenage angels
& your steel-blue Chopin martinis!

TEN MORE YEARS

God of Proust, Nabokov & D.H. Lawrence,
grant me only ten more years—that is all
I need to show off to the world that
your staggering gifts to me were not squandered
& didn't come to naught. That you are not
a spendthrift khat-chewing coot or rum sipping drunk
who revels in wasting golden nuggets to drape & bejewel
a crotchety & thankless monitor lizard like me.

SECOND COMING

God, you just thought
it would be a cinch for me
to trace your overpowering musk.

That stalking you can't be any harder
than searching for the silky-red sifaka
in big black sunglasses in wealds of Madagascar
or traipsing through Tucson's wilderness
for a grand saguaro cactus blossom
as huge as Alaska.

That you were like a grand windmill
that one could clearly gaze
from hundreds of leagues
or a dazzling diamond white abbey
against a dancing field of lavender
or perhaps you wishfully presumed
that you were brilliant as a shark
thundering between thousands of crystal jellies,

or you were an African giraffe
craning over a lake of grazing wild beasts
or were a lovely gazelle sun-tanning
in a lagoon of yellow daisies
or a titanium-bright polar bear
seal-pup-grazing in arctic wastes

but, dear God, it has been
a holy pain to telescope your furtive lights,
fogs have obscured your silhouettes
& made me nervous like magpies
& now the evening is getting
pretty kelp-dark to follow your spoors,
your tender pugmarks.
Maybe I should just chill out
by the pianissimo creek & listen
to a Bob Dylan tape or a Liszt symphony
& leave this daunting task of ferreting you out
for my second coming?

TODAY, I AM JESUS FOR A CHANGE

I no longer want to be a jester or a bartender
so today, I am Jesus for a change.
I keep his orchid eloquence, his short temper
of Kublai Khan, his bacchanal gall to declare myself—
Kama-god on roller-blades
& in hibiscus tinged silk shirt.
I die for nobody's sins or scarlet letter.
I elegantly sow my own wild oats
as long as the Viagra lasts
& when I am sated & all my sins have fruited
into red-apple groves, I persuade God
to die for my sins if he really thinks
crucifixion is a bowl of cherries.
There is after all a first time for everything.
By the way, when God is crucified,
I need no redemption or heavenly housing.

YOUR SILENCE

God, we had to fill this world with so much
cacophony & songfests glowing
like the blossoms of blue Jacaranda
because your silence was so deafening.
Of course the merry roulades of sedge wrens,
the trills of kinglets, ballads of indigo buntings
& song-webs of wood thrushes
did also share our sweet burdens.

FOR EVERY KNOTWEED RUBY PEAK

For every knotweed ruby peak baptized
by dawn's waters & for every flashy
yellow-violet-scaled queen angel fish
that you have graced my eyes with,
God Almighty, I will pen a stanza as plumed & radiant
& ruby-flecked & torch-flowery
to show you what I can do with the paltry gifts
you bestowed upon me begrudgingly
& how I have braided those teeny benedictions
into minor miracles as picturesque
as the exquisite calligraphy
on acacia trees in the plains of Serengeti.

THE FALL COLORS

Lord God, what did I do so recently
to be rewarded more ravishingly
than Watteau & Constable?

These swell museums of hues in leaves—
salmon pink, apricot-orange, Iceplant scarlet,
the smoky chiffon blues
as the dusky lapis grapes,
the hot magenta of laced lingerie
that suits my latest beloved.

Lord God, where did you intern
to paint the heaving leaves in the colors
of muslin moths & gilt monarchs,
in the quivering tints of coral reefs so perfectly?

Do these puckered-lipped leaves know
how fawned over they are,
that your splendor can write itself out
on tender scrolls like them?

Lord God, there was no plangent need
to drag a stumbling Christ bleeding
like pink orchids up to the cross
to keep us pining for your lofty scent.

The wine-red flurries of maple leaves
in Vermont were good enough
to choir your evergreen glory!

WISTFULNESS

Who knows whose poem's wings
will break a century's barrier
& rouse a virgin's narcissus breasts
but one tries one's hardest best
to fill the seething wine-press of radiance
& hope that someday one's poem
will soar like a starling & reach those velvet eyes
of violet irises, those darling alabaster hands
quivering as bridal candles.

LIKE A VIOLA

God, you have played me like a viola
for all these years transforming me
into jade fugues, lavender-blue
crocus sonatinas,
you have wafted this dusky richness
of my soul in the air
like the gilt leaves fleeing the winter

but for whose enchantment & lucky luster?
I never saw any eyes or hearts pining
for my serenades
or you just did all that busy bowing
to drown out your own deafening silence
or because you didn't know what to do
with your fretful fingers
& the music that wafted from me
becalmed your squirrel nerves
& caressed you till you got
a good night's sleep!

WHAT GOOD IS MY RICHNESS?

God, what will I do with these cascading
poems like the looming pink pods
on a tamarind tree
or the hundred ruby eggs
of a mantis shrimp
when I am living
in a country with boldly posted
billboard signs—
"Dare to hatch only if you are
a blonde crustacean."

God, what should I do with this neon magic
by which I can flash hues
from my breathtaking palette
like a flamboyant cuttlefish
when my poetry readings fill
no more than a dozen seats?

Palace Of Rimbaud

The poet makes himself a seer by a long, prodigious, and rational disordering of all the senses. Every form of love, of suffering, of madness; he searches himself, he consumes all the poisons in him, and keeps only their quintessences.

—Arthur Rimbaud

TIME & US

Why fight, beloved, who did right
& who went wrong?

Who kept his grin & who tear-drowned.

This is the gist of our story
that rang out in violet oak-glades:

That we bartered some dusks
& traded some dawns
to embellish our melancholies.

We lapped up our grappas & sipped our
Tequila sun-crests with a softer frown
& as the evenings blushed our cheeks
we ruffled some feathers
& undid some thongs

but the river never stopped
to let us take its racing pulse
& even though we waded its deep
pellucid waters like black necklaced swans
it kept moving on, it kept gliding on.

It seems, beloved, the river never belonged
& yet we grabbed some precious moments
to sing our silly love-songs
to share our lily-pink heartbreaks
to sob our soggy farewells
& then we were as quickly gone
as we came.

THE GRAVE

What difference does it make
if my grave is hewn in Rosetta stones
or limned on flapping sand dunes
or festooned on a rapid's hull
or floated in midair
like a dragnet of butterflies
or if it is a ladder in the vein-mottled sky
dotted with blue birds.

If I don't live in your hearts & eye-looms
& in your blushing dreams
I am nowhere & endlessly homeless.

LAST TANGO IN AUSCHWITZ

I can not alter the sullen
Dalmatian skies.
Snow is piled high
like the pealed tongues,
the gouged eyes,
the piles of watches, necklaces
& wedding rings.

The locked winds are loosened as egrets.
There are no hours left
for self-pity or God-loathing.

For years I taught strings
at Prague Conservatory
so let me play a hot tango
on my violin for my ibis-red requiem.

Perhaps tomorrow or the day after
I will too levitate as Northern ravens
bolting from the smoking chimneys
against the leis of poppy-white clouds.

TWO GHAZALS

I

What did the curt breeze whisper to the red-maple?
There were tear-wreathes over the grass-blades.
You were always co-traveler of sunny seasons.
Why would you come running in my darkling straits?
All we saw was crimson lights stabbing the heavens.
Staccato sirens & screams syncopated the air-raids.
They never tasted Arizona's rose-cactus aridness.
Those folks were raised by emerald everglades.

Why these doubts about your disarming beach beauty?
You would surely best Stanford's doe-eyed mermaids.
Lets drink from those Mali-blue eyes till dawn flares.
Lets lap those verbena lips before the beauty fades.
She was already taken, how could I tell that sultry angel—
"I love you more than cattleya blossoms & palm-dates."
Why this mantilla of swarthy clouds?
Haven't I braved more harrowing raids?

We sent mogra buds for Beauty's splendid braids.
Then why were we greeted with wide-shut gates?
Why Zaigham this brouhaha about penning ghazals.
Didn't you claim Meer & Faiz as your playmates?

II

You might surmise I am lavishly insane
begging you to call on me again & again?
I bled with bliss after many searing summers.
Beloved: You were such ravishing dew-flowery rain.
Whether the town is flooded or goes up in flames,
she doesn't care—that crooning, fox trotting train!
How one craves to own their airborne gears,
How one envies those white thundering cranes.

I can recount all the minuets of that lush evening,
but why did I forget the legato of a dear refrain?
Who will care at all in scores of years about
the cadenzas of my sqill wins & glory-lily gains?
To weave an intoxicating furze ghazal, beloved,
pray tonight for some exquisite sea lavender pains.

A FATAL ANGINA

The courtyard fount blazed
as a crystal lotus by Chihuly.
The waft of the purple-red
hydrangea blossoms blushed the air.
I had just poured you some
deep blackberry cabernet.
A frond of light gleamed your mane.
Your eyes were wide shut
cuddling the prelude of raga Kalavati.
How blissful I was in your orchid spell;
then why, beloved, did death brazenly started
crooning her maudlin aria & by the time
it finally halted we were splintered forever?

DESPERATELY SEEKING IMMORTALITY

Beloved: why must I crave immortality
as the fire moth covets a candle's tongue
or a deer pines for penstemon blossoms
when a yen for eternal is nowhere scrolled
on your short roster of longings!

END OF OFFICE ROMANCE

So we have decided, beloved,
that we will avoid each other as the faun
shuns the foxgloves, that we will live
in the nearby cubicles but behave
as if we were total strangers
& never owned each other,
never shared the same heart beats
or formed an oasis of colors.
That our bodies were never woven
in the quilt of a tight rapture,
& we never gazed at the stars together
& felt we were eternal. That our lips never
delved in kisses that felt endless as summer rains,
that our longings are now forever detoured & channeled
to other cheek-candles, other songbirds—
buddleja-eyes, taffy lips & Erica-pink shoulders.

Whose Pleasure?

Don't ask me what is a *Pietà* or a peacock-ginger blossom
or a sumptuous Delacroix noon or Klimt evening
or what aquarium of stars means
with that curled, half-sneering lip of yours,
with that sophomoric Dubya twinkle.
I am not here to dazzle your dung-beetle
butchers, cowhands, roofers, reefer-floated
cab drivers, prisoners of 12-packs, rattle-snake
wife beaters & born-haters of books.
I am here to pleasure the gypsy ghosts
of Rimbaud, Hafiz & Josh.
Any swallowtail heartthrobs that ever lived,
any heliotrope vanilla/cherry pie scented
flower head & pansy orchid raptures that were
ever conjured up by shamans like me
I will freely use to give the thrills
of firecrackers to my poetry's lark-bunting heart.

To me great poetry is a Moroccan meadow
dappled with wild irises, lilacs, poppies' blush,
crush of cherry trees, prickly Barbary figs
& red wooded firs. Remember,
I am not a fisherman's bastard.
I am Mallarmé 's scion,
Octavio Paz's next door neighbor.
To me opulence is God's gay hairdresser,
It is Apollo's foxy masseur.
It is the Toa arbor, it is Trinity's triple blossom,
the tiki torch in Brahma's head,
the flamenco kniphofia dancing in my garden.

Don't Ask Me

How a couture silk magenta dress can't help
rubbing against the full fire-lily curves
of Adriana Lima? Don't ask me how hard
it was for me not to fall in love with a woman
who was as handsome as a flowering
blue meconopsis with a central fuzz
of golden yellow stamens & who penned
poems as lucent & smoky as Diana Krall's ballads.

LIKE THE DIVA AT THE ORCHESTRA HALL

The humble, lowborn, lowbrow insufferable lines
that feud like lurid Crips & Bloods
to get an upper hand will finally lose out
to the last stanza in a dazzling poem

as if a diva has just been flown in
from Milan or Madrid
who doesn't need the props
of sheet music to caste spells—
like a spotlight her exuberance drives out
all the huddled voices in a penumbral arch
& when she belts her gorgeous aria
& pitches it towards the carousel of the stars
the sleepy Olympians wake up with a start,

Duke Ellington winks like a diamond watch,
Louis Armstrong flashes his 14-carat grin,
the snazzy concertmaster, the nervous impresario,
the moon-bald conductor
with long eye lashes & ferocious gestures,
the cosseted mermaids
in the baroque isles & wings,
the gargoyles & angels perched on walls
become the glorious fixtures of a staggering mural
as if shepherded by Fra Angelica.
Multiple gunshots are fired
at the pearl ribcage of eternity
& polyrhythmic fruits of gold, rubies
& lavender gaiety are burst open
& swinging blood croons & preens
& kicks heels as if Lord Shiva
is serving up a sizzling Bharatnatyam!

NIGHT BURNS IN MY BLOOD

Night burns in my blood like the rings of Jupiter
or is it you, beloved, in a lilac décolletage
that I can't drink or touch & can only sing
& dream of & introduce to my buddies
& the bartender as my part-time muse.

THE ENVY OF THE GREAT

She tells me—what is the moot point
of your penning so many exuberant poems,
ornamental like pink shower trees & immortelles
if you can't out-gleam Rilke or Ghalib?
Let's spend remains of our days
globe-trotting, bird watching or scuba diving
in Belize & the Cayman Islands,
there, we have a decent chance
to hold a candle to those radiant angels
so I tell her—darling, we all must do
those uncanny things

that give us greatest gleaming.
Shakespeare didn't fuss over
if he surpassed Dante
or if he bested Homer's game
after limning *Hamlet* & *King Lear*.
Our genius must sing till its chords break.
All ripened quinces must still
be prized like a crown prince.
They must be picked & glazed
even if they are not the envy
of the royal table.

BETWEEN WISDOM & BEAUTY

Between Nietzsche's sparkling wisdom
& the pastel palette of a male anthias
with its deep green eyes, lavender-red
mantle & gold dappled fins,

I will always choose the fabulous anthias
because its wonder doesn't pale
or mutate over time between
sublime & ridiculous
as Nietzsche's electro flashes could
for my heart's aquarium.

BURIAL INSTRUCTIONS

When you prepare me for Osiris

plant me under the candelabra of an oak sapling
& the violet cascade of stars.

I would love a reed of petrified
wood standing at my stone head,
an angel counting down the noons remaining

till resurrection's big ball.

A sprig of dried sage
latched by a lavender cockade

would be splendid & flapping accompaniment
to the westerly wind's impromptu crooning.

On the façade of my redwood coffin,
I would much prefer the ballet of tulips
& butterflies in vertiginous drifts

& if it is not too much of a bother,
instead of a silver cross on my breast

I would love to carry gilt pendants
with images of Rimbaud & Lorca,
favorite saints to warm my heart.

The lambent rains have little clue
that I have loved these two
ghosts more fondly

than the breast-baring sorority girls
on Bourbon Street,
that I love those saints more than
Casablanca's last scene
when Bogart makes Ingrid Bergman leave
the looming hell without him.

LANGUAGE AS CARIBANA FEST

America, I am tired
of watching my words
being spare, circumspect,
canny, straitjacketed.

I want my phrases to dance
the salsa, the conga, the calypso,
the tango, the bossa nova,
the hora, the cha-cha, the tarantella.

I want my lines to prance & shimmer
in masquerade,
grace the magical floats,
rattle the heaven's gates.

I adore those foxy words with breasts
re-touched, re-sculpted
to double up the raptures,

tummies tucked, thighs, hips, buttocks
toned & liposucted, lips curled
for kisses to perch like hummingbirds
& reminisced for entire summers,

I love zonked brazen words
with mascara-flecked eyes
with starry demeanors
in hot mauve & lavender,

all decked out in brocades,
beaded silks & pearls
controlling the traffic
as the fabulous
feathered girls
do in a totally sinful &surreal
Caribana Fest in Toronto.

MISTY WATCHING

The cat strolls sleuth-like in the cavern
of our spit clean basement.
She reminds me of a little silly girl, I spied on,
tiptoeing around her ancestral hut
in a Sindhi village
looking for a doll or a felled mango.
The cat is unrelenting,
unsparing as a pirate.
With her butterfly paws,
she frisks the long stripes
of the king size mattress,
the languishing hulk
of the brocaded maroon sofa chair
waiting for a second christening.

She scales up to the glazed
cupboard's ceiling
& devoutly squats in the bare pews
of the empty bookcase.
She rushes through her sweet hymns
with a hint of evangelical flair
but she is mostly playful like an otter,
her rump caresses the cold translucence
of the oblong window pane.
She holds her breath to take in
the diasporic ballad of the wild geese.
She is a twee eunuch, all tied up, sown in.

Her nipple-moons will never ooze
with milk, motherhood or raptures.
No dating, no nuptials, no heartbreaks.
But she will keep faking as if all that
didn't happen & she is so thrilled to be
Saint Claire or Saint Theresa
in the annals of her species.
I see her wrestle with
the knee-knocked exercise bike,
her tinsel whimpers & twangs tease,
the cerulean silence of the place,
her voice sows it with mauve silk threads.

She prances, rages, heaps
meowed invectives at spider's filmy web
& carries off the tangled gossamer
on her pretty mane & countenance
& after becoming disgusted
she spits out & dawdles
by the staircase—bald, carpet-less.
She stands upright, a picador
against the spine of the furnace.
The lance of the grass-pea blue
pubic flame rivets her fancy,
then she clambers the omnibus
of my son's rainbow slide
& stretches & flays her tufted limbs
like a foxy bar room stripper
in her seedy glory.

She nods approvingly
at the water level in the sump-pump,
running her paws over the heating ducts
& being so close to the insulating
butter-weed canopy
she reaches out for the jutting elephant ears.
Her reckless bravado earns her my chiding.
but the cat is super slick.
She unrolls herself like a gilded leaf
of an exquisite book to be massaged all over.

You can tell that she is all Id, all pleasure,
all Madonna, all Brigitte Bardot.
I give her a body rub
till she purrs as Huron harbor
& then she makes a lazy drop
& goes to a dark corner
still somewhat amethyst
she studies her looming shadow
of a mountain loin cub & wonders
if the silhouette is indeed
the fawning rain-lily ghost
of an ancestor blessing her.

BEAUTY'S WORDS

Beloved: I hang on to every sepal,
anther & pistil of your words
like the admiring buttes cling
to every petal of the flowering dusk
as if wishing to glean
as many swirling blossoms
as they can of its arabesque splendor.

THE STORM

Yes, the storm still rages
as memory flips its pages
& gets knotted in glinty images
of your auburn locks
& violet eyes that could
lift me with the tenderness
of ginger lilies
but today it makes my face roil
in a whirlpool of stars.

HIS DADDY'S GIFTS

Beneath the heavy patina of this
unstoppable colossus
who had easily penned
some five hundred cherry blossom poems,
I can scratch off the glossy sheen
& can make out the silhouette
of an Uttar Pradeshi lad
barely six in khaki boxer shorts
& without an undershirt quivering
like a leaf inhaling as an asthmatic
his old man's violent rage who as he
staggered in the clammy tenement
from his drunken spree almost each week
had the absolute power to halt
that little boy's fluttering cardinal heart
with one deadly scream & had almost succeeded
but the kid magically survived to write
some five hundred poems—one each
for his daddy's every awkward try
to put out his tender flame.

THE KABUL OF MY POETRY

The stratagem here, dear reader is not
to crush you under the scaffolding
of my high-brow phrasing
or to coerce you
with heavy posturing & strut
of a menacing warlord
with hashish-red eyes,
AK-47 assault-rifle
& a beaded eye-catching bandolier
but to seduce you entirely
with the blazing poppy fields
of my cantos & steal you away
from other name brand poetry cartels.

BEAUTY AS THE ASSASSIN

Who could have guessed
that beauty had an assassin's heart
to parcel a lover's oleander tongue
in a gold salver to crescendo
my ever cresting hunger for her?

SOME PREREQUISITES FOR FRIENDSHIP

If you were as much a vaudeville phenom
as the African gray parrot
with a paprika-red tail
& chutzpah of a sage & a sadhu
or if you were as sweet & gregarious
as the Bernice Mountain bitch
with black velvet pelt, golden brown legs,
& diamond-white neckline or haply
if you were as charismatic
as a Catalina Macaw with resplendent
orange breast, emerald-green wings
& Picasso-dabbled, latticed over-cheeks
or if you were as debonair as the Abyssinian
pepper & salt Colobus monkey

I could have considered befriending you.

THE ENIGMA OF ARRIVAL

When death finally makes
its frantic touchdown
will it rumble like a Boeing 757
or will it drop in like the splashy crash landing
of the scarlet-footed sea birds?
Will I feel like a hapless bat caught in midair
by an emerald boa constrictor
& I will have no prayer?
Will I be like a nervous squid
hunted by an emperor penguin?
Will death rattle my every string
like an old reviled sitar
or will it jab me cold & senseless
with a single, knock out jolt?

Will it come all decked out with the jewelry
of needles, ivy drips, struts, frets of tubes,
scaffold of straitjacket, stanchions
& dripping nipples of morphine
or will it simply play with me for hours
like Samantha in *Sex & The City*
& fellate me so tenderly
that I would never wake up
from the shock of multiple orgasms?
Will it be majestic like a Daiquiri-red sunset
or will it be spectral like a nightscape
in a siren-draped air bombed Beirut?

Will it sweetly whisper my name
like Carrie Underwood cooing
her melancholy summer ballad
or will it detonate my ears
like the thundering strains
of a Rolling Stones apocalypse?

Will it spit out all the pretty
moon-jellyfish memories
or will it launch them on the big radar screen
of my exploding thalamus
for hours long horrid eternities?

Will it punish my wife & my two kids
by staging my grand jitters & convulsions
or will it spare them the gory contortions
& pyrotechnics as the great courtesy of a Houdini-God?
Will it break my voice & I will lose my grace
or would it be like a soft mizzle donning
a magenta blue vest in its aster tenderness?
Will I vomit & sweat profusely
as if I had a can of jalapeno
or would it leave me faintly fragrant
like a sprig of deep-rose celosias?

Will I be well-schooled by then in the art of dying
or will I behave like a spoiled kindergarten kid
yelling & dragging my feet at every rip & slit?
Will it embrace me like the blushing breeze
caressing the cool camellias & after
the long drawn hug I shall flutter no more?

DESPAIR

Beloved, you were
every inch those hula girl hibiscus blossoms,
those bashful yellow forsythia buds,
those fretful coral-red fuchsias,
those grinning saffron crocuses,
those lavender viola blooms
coquettish beyond their tender age.

Since you have deserted me
for that lousy half-wit rapper & part-time bouncer,
what use do I have now
for the waft of those flowers
or their catchy blaze or clairvoyance—

they all remind me
of your maddening scents & hues.

One might just as well, beloved,
burn down the garden!

AN ELEGY'S RESONANCE

If beauty never stopped
to savor her praises, dear heart
we can still be proud
that we did our best
to float her splendor,

Didn't we lavishly keened
for her emerald eyes
like other lovers wailed
for the green cedars of Zion?

Perhaps she was too time-pressed
to requite our affections,
but it must be plenty
that our laments' refrains
were often resonant through
the ruby-blushed hills.

ADVICE TO A FLEDGLING POET

Poetry must lap you like a marsh tern.
It must nibble you like a sparrow hawk.
It must lick your nipple-buds till you roil
with a scut erection.
It must singe you like a flame
till your tears run over, it must keep you sleepless
at night like a night watchman.
It must make you steal from Titian's grave
& Cleopatra's charm-chest
for its urgent makeup & embellishments.
If it doesn't do all these riveting things to you,
You must do something thing else.
You'd be no good husband to poetry.

THE SHEAF

America: take this hibiscus
sheaf of my poems
& feel its mohair suppleness & marvel
how a neglected & shut out poet ached
to see them hug the firm arches
of your Alpine aster breasts.

No Midnight-Gold Thongs, Please

No, I don't want you to hand me
a cutout from your black
rhinestone camisole

or a scorching fringe from your
cascading auburn locks
to insinuate how many gasps & wings
my poems have given you.

Nor I want you to pass me the electric keys
of your hotel suite overlooking
the Waikiki beach to send me off
with multiple penstemon raptures—
scarlet & soft as sparrow's tongue
as you surely would
for Mr. Tom Jones or Mr. Billy Joel.

Nor I wish you to nearly rip off your
plum-lace brassiere at my sight
like you would for a born again
Casanova or a grinning Tom Cruise.

I just want you to telegraph through your
flame vine gestures that I can read so fluently:
when my poems caress you gently
like sips of sparkling prosecco
on a summer noon
you are so completely enchanted
that you feel as if you never knew till now

how language could be so nimble,
so fluid like Pavlova dancing Giselle,
so winsome & flickering
like purple-throated mountain gem,
so gilt & surf-blue in its hushed
beachside raptures,
so handsome like a flycatcher
in his flashy green-blue tuxs.

LIKE A VERMEER

America, I will douse you
with bucket-loads
of my high-octane exuberance
till you are dripping wet & brazen
like a Brazilian super model
in a see through bikini
& then I will set you blazing
in acacia-tall flames
of my sizzling verses
till you start screaming
like an amped up rocker
that you have now tasted
Solomon's cestrum opulence,
that you now realize how
David's harp could wow
prophet Saul & a sorority hall
brimming with sultry freshwomen,
that you can now dig
how Moses tripped
when the famous bush
gunned his sights.

That you can now fully endorse
the famous miracle that the moon was halved
like a melon when the prophet
wagged his finger at her.

That Lazarus came back from the dead
meringue dancing to lap amber-colored
Guyana rum because you have
already witnessed quite often
how language would lay bare
before this swarthy bard
like a magic canvas on which
he could paint star rose
dreams like Vermeer.

THE IMPOSTER

Oh! Solomon I have surpassed thee.
          —Suleyman the Magnificent

He always bragged if given the chance
he could gallantly show as a latter-day Vasari
how Marlowe must have sketched
Helen's aster countenance & its Rococo sadness.
He would boast like a rooster how he could
limn as Rubens the lumbering fleets & triremes
holding back torrents of half-famished Greek soldiers
storming over to avenge Helen's honor.

That he could interpret so deliciously
in meticulous ballet steps how Gauguin's brush
might have dealt with the mahogany teenage pelts
of South Sea girls with all their feral epiphanies.

He crowed so ravishingly that he could savor
on his palate how the amethyst caviar of greatness
must have tasted on Pushkin's vermilion tongue

or how someday he will tell off our greatest bard:
oh! sailor-humping giant I have surpassed thee
in exuberance by at least a hundred meters
& now suddenly he has been given the chance
to prove his Tanzanite boasts & to turn
flanks of opal crystals into blazing candelabras,
bleeding sun catchers, thundering chandeliers
as if he is now commissioned
to distill cherubs & nymphs

from thin blue Rockies air
but he seems too headlong, too overwhelmed.
His parasol head is in a tailspin.
His eyes keep failing him in tracing the foggy contours
in translucent marble & his fickle hands quake like ferns
unwilling to deliver the ambrosia bowls,
the liqueur wares, the long overdue Fabergés
of greatness as if he is going to be
revealed soon for the rank imposter he always has been.

CHANGING OF THE GUARDS

Son, my eyes jiggle with stars
when I watch how the stage-lights
lap up your Adonis face
like votive candles pining for calla lilies.

How your lava-blushed cheeks
gleam as primrose candies,

how your long eyelashes
give me a sudden gasp & spring,

how your thick Moorish mane haloes
your diamond-cut handsomeness,

how the silver bough
of your trumpet swings
in your cherub hands
dripping ballads like finches
on apple blossoms,

how your eyes & brows slow-dance
those Miles Davis riffs,
how music becomes your silhouette,
lilac-red & arabesque,

how your chestnut eyes
that grasped the subtle points
in *A Short History Of Time* at age nine,
measure up the chatty audience,

how your snow goose lyre breast
seems awashed in a meteors shower
or in a mizzle of pale pearls.

Son, you now borrow daddy's shoes & shirts
for your jazz concerts & dance clubs
& you are still growing & pushing hard
the restless envelope.

I, an old lynx caught in an awesome snare,
don't think you really understand
why I am under such crumping stress,

how I am melting like a sizzling coil
in some livid Chernobyl,

how I am giddy as a sand hill crane
by a bubbling sunset

& God who locked up my eloquence
for twenty-two years now wishes
to make up for his long absences.

The rabid rain of his kindness
is now endless but I can no longer
endure its ramming pulse;

I am choking by the fumes of his blessings.

Son, with your impish ubiquitous gaze
& marbled arms of a teenage Apollo

you are better suited than your father
to carry this cross of belated grace,

this thundering arc
of latter-day incandescence,
down the steepled bluffs.

Sweetheart, this burden is better suited
for a jolly teenager who can grin & scuff
like a mauve lavandulas

while playing a gorgeous etude
or humming a Sinatra tune
while hustling his SAT test

& one who can schlep & drag
a thirty-pound rucksack
almost daily to Novi High.

THE SUGAR MAPLE TREE

You, a carousal of catbirds & you rock
like a suave mumbo dancer.
You a chartreuse harp
strumming itself.
My strident, gunmetal epic poems
are teeny bamboo shoots
when played next to your pearl murmurs.
Oh! the sailboat of blue jays & cardinals,
the great heartbreak hotel of yellow warblers
gate keeper of Amaranthus bushes
casting purple veils & lavish spells.

Oh! the sentry of flowering crab apple trees,
a voyeur of a coy eternity blow drying
her cosmos, crocus, cyclamen bras,
a thespian who has taken vows of silence
but now is winning raving reviews
for his mimed eloquence.
Thousands of turquoise eyes swell
in your upwardly sweeping stairwells.
Who would look at the fake flicker of streetlamps
or the sham beauty of mannequins
barely dressed against your jewelry of jade.

Temple, Ferris wheel, onion-breasted mosque
all hum under the tower bell
of your enormous breast.
Oh! palace of mazes, strip mall
of catwalks & bridges,
your playfulness overturns my kayak of sadness
like a sea running over baby sea lions.
Your arms & forehead ooze with thousand tines.
You, the great archangel watching over
the armies of spider orchids & parrot tulips,

o giddying plenum, o fecundity's sweetness,
is your sudden stillness Sidharta's fierce silence
or is it like Lord Krishna's plotting
another ruse, another blushing stratagem
against the gorgeous lake-bathing gopies?

THE APOTHEOSIS OF VICTOR HUGO

His chamber had a frontal view
of the Champs-Elysées,
which was an outright spectator nuisance
& a vulgar rapture like New Orleans.

The chamber reeked of charred-sweetness
of expensive cigars
& liquor bottles he had stashed
in his redwood desk just in case
some handsome gazelle admirer
might tiptoe in his well-cluttered chamber
at an odd hour & murmur

for an aperitif or whisky sour
before they made love on his mahogany desk.
His books were scattered like shot birds
in Synders' *Still life with poultry & venison.*

The windows had bled that noon
by a spring shower with fulgurous diamonds.
His caramel blues were not much cured
by nature's fireworks or by the vase
of fresh penstemons & jacquinias

or by his favorite cod *Goujonnettes*
& the *soupe à l'Oignon* that lay cold & un-favored.

Till this hour, though hugely gifted
& sought after, he was
just a workaholic virtuoso
not completely sure of his shaky destiny,
one who jealously watched with awe
like a fawning trapeze artist
the dizzying power swoops,
the precipitous drops & hoops
in one-man ballets
of Dumas, Balzac & Sainte-Beauve.

Half hour into the afternoon
he suddenly felt tethered by a numinous light
grasping him like a desperate lover
who wouldn't let go off his arms.
He felt scared like a doe drizzling with sweat,
his heart raced as a derby horse.
An eerie voice echoed
from within like a Delphic oracle.

From now on, Victor,
you are the rose window
through which divine lightnings
will thunder through to glory France,

that you are no longer
the caricature of greatness,
that your hands are no more
some plebian appendages,
now interned to Zeus & Apollo,
you will now see what the gods rake
with their radium eyes,

that you no longer need your lover's lips
or begonia breasts to savor grace.

You are henceforth the raging kiln
in which eternity's terracotta
will glow like passiflora,
like belladonna's blossoms,
like angel's breath.

Despite epiphany's noir fringe
he felt relieved as if
a boulder had been lifted off his chest.

He silently wept for the fey blessing.

Two days later Balzac was dead

& Victor Hugo was one of the pallbearers.

A FAKE ROLEX SWAGGER

For art to exist, for any sort of aesthetic activity to exist,
a certain physiological precondition is indispensable: intoxication.
                              —Friedrich Nietzsche
But in the instance of Ali, this veneration carried over into actual deification,
so that Ali was represented as an incarnation of God.
                    —Martin Kramer—*Shi'ism, Resistance, and Revolution*

Give us your meek, your wimpy,
your acrophobic, dilettante & stay safe poets
with Styrofoam jawbones & teeth.
These poets will never speak of Allende,
9/11 or Iraqi invasion & Sudanese holocaust.
We will ply them with Dante's tangerine vodka
& hundred proof gaiety & subversive cockiness & bluster.
We will bless them with the drawl
& sentimental eloquence of blue thrush,
with bougainvilleas' opulent sprawl,
scarlet sage blush & the elegance
of egret-white jasmines wafting like queens.
We, born of thigh-banging *forró*-loving seas
aren't overawed by Homer's nautical skills,
his cruising fleets, his accordion waves,
his famous derbies, his hand-painted jalopies.

If ardently begged for a poem's dash & glory
we can become jangly triangles & pretty vociferous
as deep-throated zabumba drums
but if it is plenty to be daisy-tender & lyrical
we can just ford in Yeats' supple rapids
or meet up with Gary Snyder
in Yosemite's wilderness to hold séances with sequoias,
pines, incense cedar herds over the cloud bursts
of Afghani hash & salvia-blue ghosts of Chinese bards.
Nothing in our Torah is frowned or forbidden.
We take our cues from no gods or goddesses,
we improvise daily creation' librettos & chap books
& God really digs us & sings our hymnals as if
we were his sons & daughters because we *are* his radiant
fuchsia face, his diamond stylus, his sweet bulbuls,
his calloused, un-tiring potter's hands.

THE FEARED OUTCOME

I fret a lot that I will die
before I have published
all my sprawling works
but in the grand scheme of things & Thanatos
in which skirt blooming
square dancing galaxies
swirl & blaze like sea urchins
& then fade out like alley ghosts
it doesn't matter if I even publish
a chapbook or manage to plant
two dozen opuses.
No one would fret
a thousand years from now
if I were as riveting
as Lorca or Akhmatova

& yet the itch abides & takes over
to make me plod on & write
till the wee hours of the morning
while my head starts to ring & spin
like an electro top
& I am deathly scared
that I will hemorrhage some veins
in my head & go insane like Celan or Nietzsche
or kill myself for being so overloaded
& jangled with goddess Sarasvati's
electric surge.

THE FELLED POETS

A couple of Karachi bards with whom I once shared
vaulted laughs, lovely squabbles, amaryllis jealousies
& mistresses & whom I secretly suspected
of being divinely branded & tapped to become
semi-immortals like Poe & Pasternak now luxuriantly rest
under the graying grave stones
& mists of bearded irises & blue hyacinths.
They commune with lapis rains
& clairvoyant stars & wait fretfully
for my friendly knocks as the sweet alyssums
wait for spring's welcome call.

THE DESCENT OF VIRGINIA WOOLF TO THE FLEET OF IMMORTALS

She is not scared
by the thought of subsuming waves.
She now thinks they are her chums like the stones
in her coat pockets that she has been hording
on her long walks on Rodmell streets.

She has been wading like an emperor penguin
in an exhilaration-ocean for days.
She has finished the two letters
with frenzied verve
for her girlfriend & her loyal husband

& has sealed them like fate

& placed them on piano sill by the balustrade.
She has attempted this before like a heist
but this time she would banish failure.
Her planning is perfect, she fancies,
like a well-latticed novel;

Leonard—busy for another four hours
at his printing press thinking
Virginia is writing & re-writing
a scathing note to punish the critic
who has dogged her most recent novel.
The two maids puttering about
& flurrying in the kitchen
are prepping pan-roasted salmon
in ginger-carrot butter
with rice, pistachios, currants
& stuffed hare
with chopped fennel, marjoram, sage,
thyme & rosemary in bacon fat—
two pastoral delicacies as they call them.

From her study she spies the plumes
of their gossip-tinged laughter.
Deep pockets of her winter coat
are the unopened sails
that will take her to the other shore
for which she so madly aches.

She touches their bulge with tenderness.
Her mind has been made up for weeks.
Only she can see the harrowing
urgency of her Karma.

She imagines Leonard's tear-tasseled face
at her crowded stand-only funeral.
If there is going to be one,
She thinks with a wry grin.
He has done his duty for amore
& for the implacable Kali of Art.
He needs a permanent deliverance
from the recurring nightmares
of my breakdowns.
He would eventually figure out
why this final shearing
is so very salient for all three of us.

She smiles at the imperfect gleaning of words
but there is no time for word-smithing.
"My work is up there to speak for itself."
She hears her own whispers
in the bellowing grottos of her mind.
She imagines, after the deed is done,
the yellowing phantom of the fetal moon
scaling the gasping waves hiding
her last clever plot, her last stratagem.
She is not all that mindful of the ululating
arbutus trees in the lawn
or the uddered clouds suffocating the skies.

She crosses the garden
littered with fog & foreboding
to focus on her final mission,
walks down the stairway
to the compound's periphery.
In three minutes she is ensconced
in her final circumference.
She walks towards the hectoring waters
not like a swan but as a blue-winged teal.

Her suppliant body folds
as a sprig of daffodils
to receive the lashing
saber-hands of the rapids.
The retching waves hack away
her descending chin,
the famous avian nose,
the leafy eyes, the flattened mane
more precious than all
the sitting queens of Europe.

In that weltering hour
the waters receive the eerie gift
of a skiff-body hemmed
by rotund stones.
She has birthed 31 books
but has borne no children,
loved a man & a woman
as ardently as her jealous muse
would permit. The waters have no use
for this benediction
as if she were a tired gull
who just dropped in to waddle
in violet lilies & amnesia.

There is no horror there.
No scarlet-flaxes of shame.
Just the afterglow
of a fully bejeweled life.

The bucking leviathan waves
steer her where she wishes to be—
in the limpid indigo bottom.

She has no pulse.
Her eyes are sightless stars
but her heart is still kindling & warm
as she joins the cheering fleet of immortals,

holding her un-posted reprimand for the critic—
sassy & terse in her bluing hands.

THE WRITER & HIS BIRDS

What will be his story so coddled & glamorized
that it will lose his signature damask scent
like blood washed by churning waters
so before he becomes
a funnel cloud of fibs & hot helium
swept by the profligate sadness of fogs
we must let you in on a few amusing things:
He fanatically believed in the Tao of tea.
A pot of steaming chai with sugar & cream
in early morning would buoy him like a lantern fish.
That his noons blushed as lobelia buds
whenever a blue bird flecked his house deck.
He loved gazing at the emerald shroud
of lichens & mosses loosely draping
vine maple branches in his garden.
He would shed tears of rapture looking
at an arch of red-breasted goose dappling the heavens.

He would glance at college freshwomen
in their tight T-shirts & regal breasts
& think of his college days on Madison campus
when lust grew wild as wood sorrels & bracken.
Despite his perfidious knees he would play tennis
with his favorite niece
who would let him cheat with a sage smirk.
His frets filled him like a Scottish bagpipe
without crowding out the melodies,
he with his tatterdemalion falsetto would sing
Urdu ghazals to his amused children.
He brazenly stole epithets & grimaces
from bartenders & testy waitresses
more often than from Baudelaire or Emerson.
His fickleness towards God was so hilarious.
He would be rooting for him in the morning
& cursing him soundly by the evening
& despite his daunting backaches & dizzy spells
he gallantly rode his loquacious books
to the finish lines. He often rehearsed his final
death-dive in his muddled head like terns
dart-diving in arctic waters.

IN PRAISE OF SUBLIME SELFISHNESS

We poets are what we are:
the gilding eyes of mountain gods,
the jasmine wafts, the lilac flares,
the parrot-fishes often rare.

So stop bugging me, daughter, by nagging me
to send another money order
to this trusted charity or to that Indian orphanage
as a token for my infamous
bleeding heart liberal democrat piety.
You tell me that my time is frantically short
before the winged-hangman
would tighten his cords.

You urge me to go teach the inner city kids
some reading & writing skills
to earn some merit in Allah's eyes
& I tell you: sweetheart,
the silver blue stars owe us nothing
but only the faint flicker of their azure blaze,
the mauve-flushed robinas
& purple-lipped laelias owe us only
their lurid aromas & the mantid-green seas
are only beholden to us
for the raptures of peacock flounders
& blue-green tobies.

Daughter, I owe nothing to this world
except my staves' flaming trumpets
& my cantos' cinnabar rhododendrons
If you catch me sleeping on my job
you can call me the big bad cheat & loafer
& watch my debts to the world & God
start mounting like sand hills.

Till then daughter let's keep it quiet
& not make it so hard for me to write.

A Poet's Duty

By doing his vows for Keats & scarlet sage,
a poet never forsakes
his right to be outraged
against keener injustices.

He has to howl & weep & take umbrage
with the rest of the human race
if that is all that he can muster
otherwise he should show up
by the blazing barricades
with his angry gun
to prove that he is willing
to kill & be blasted
for things bigger than his celosia diction,
more urgent than his cocaine fix, more heart-kindling
than his groupie-garden or kids & his often paraded
premonitions of immortality.

Mr. Wordsworth's Planet

What you surmised so feverishly,
nostalgically & glowingly,
Mr. Wordsworth, in the lilac-quiver
of a monarch butterfly,
in the crimson blotches on a cobalt fire-eel,

in the ballad of a blue finch
longing for a rainbow-balcony
or in the sweetness of a calyxed mouth
still gasping in the afterglow of a deep kiss

were not really
the tinkling intimations
& ciphers of immortality
you imagined you have lost for ever.

Those sightings, my dear friend, were in fact
your own heart's tremors, trills, rhapsodies & prayers

writ loud & large like Jupiter's stars
over the nervous strings of creation's harpsichord.

A Short Reading

If I could read all the legions of my work,
I wouldn't stop, maybe, for three weeks
but the flame & the flicker of my breath
would give out thankfully in the first hour;
but today, this half-hour should be enough
to whip up the lupinus ruse.
Here in full display are a few silhouettes
of a veritable jinn who hungered more often
for myrtle metaphors & metaphysics
than revelations & women's midriffs,
who sang the praises of language
as if it were more wondrous
than coral reefs & Adriana Lima's breasts,
who never saw the subtle difference
between death & poetry.
To him, both were breathtakingly majestic,
hypnotic, necromantic, crimson as convallaria bells,
frantic as the ambling typhoons
& vastly ravenous as the stampeding sea.

How He Became A Writer

He had learnt at the ripe old age of eight
that in order to mask a tiny lie
one had to fabricate a more trellised
& captivating one. He was warned that it is how
dictators & priests prevailed by steady crops of holier
& more riveting lies & embellishments.
As he grew bolder with time & learnt how to swing & Charleston
on the gyre of the world, how to take its crazy pulse,
his lies mushroomed like
the swan-stirred crinkled waves in a whirlpool.
He figured that all literary masterworks
belonging to a higher order of lies & innuendoes
were fretworks of fibs lightly garnished
with attractive facts to aid the digestion.
Thus by leaping from one feebler lie-perch
to a more compelling one he became finally
a full-bodied writer—unfatigued & over-proud
in the art of counterfeiting though nobody said
a mighty one like Mann or Rushdie!

Let Night Be The Granite Stone

Let night be the granite stone
for my amorphous makeshift grave.
I love the open vistas & the constant scene changes
served up by Stonehenge clouds.
Let the ever open canopy of the salvia-blue skies
act as my grand diorama.
Let the spurt of comets bestow me
with the tame fireworks I always rooted for.
Let the fireflies weave a cape of stars
over my open eyes & vaulted ribs.
Let the wildflowers rustled by the dervish winds
dance off the moving feast of scents.
Let's not be silly or narcissistic
so don't wall me in from my real friends
by cloistering me in a tomb.
I am not some pompous Dante
to be fussed over & onion-domed.
Let me court the conga rains,
the chrysanthemum tiaras of Pikes Peak.

Let the birds of prey feast
on my tangy sarcous & scrotum.
Let them enjoy a free banquet on my till.
Don't hire poor Mexicans from the streets
to mumble prayers for me.
Let the widowed westerly wind
commiserate & lisp the needed prayers.
Let the staid moon, trusted friend for years,
be my sentry, let my remains be soaked
every evening by a dusk shower.
Let the knobby ends of my femur & flat top
of the tibia serve as the giant
conference tables for the insects & the birds.
Let my bones look milky like bellflowers in the shimmer
of moon's sawdust, let the sun dye the bones
golden as it gilds the ocean & the watercress green
mountains, Let the children use my polished skull
to spout blasphemies against gods & tyrants.
Let the angels play chess against the winds
with my seasoned bones & win a few.

RILKE IN DISTRESS

Nothing has really changed in my galaxy—
the daily drip of three hypertensive meds
or my diurnal pilgrimage to the neighborhood Y;
my ascetic diet too remains as salubriously boring
as it was in the last quarter,
my sleep is still on an even-keel,
no sea change from my steep investments
in things immanent & metaphysical
nor I have taken up smoking or pumped anabolic steroids
to cut down on my sexual craving
or inflict testicular atrophy.

I haven't hooked up on Meth or angel dust
to sauce up my raptures,
haven't smoked freebased coke since college
but something has wrapped a big ice pack
around my erotic tulip;
Is it my age finally catching up
with my limp sex pistol or is it
the selfish shrew of my writing
that won't let go my heart
for another sexy belle?

MY POEMS

Dear daughter: Don't dog my poems
like the stale kiwifruit sushi
made with smoked salmon
& poached shrimps
just because my verses don't fit in
with your J. Lo & Janet Jackson taste.

My poems are the only stardust of my ashes
that will shimmer like fire moths
till the end of your days
& if you show a little bit
of kingfisher's patience
my poems may even twitter to you
like your cheeping toddler
in magnolia diapers.

RESURRECTIONS & FACSIMILES

The shocked Madonna in an ivory
duchesse satin dress who had
no premonition or clairvoyance
that she was now my official muse,
the sabbatical God often tattooed
in my poetry's heavens
whose caress was never felt
or the lavish rains that never came
that I promised to my doubting tribe
were only the amethyst phantoms
blow-glassed by a nostalgic heart
always craving for revivals, resurrections
of its lost raptures,
its vanished elegies & the frayed denims
of its fevered prayers.

ALL MY VICES

Think of it, dear reader,
how privileged you have been
being the principal beneficiary
of all my verbal geode transgressions,
as if you are stealing the afterglows
of a hundred deflowered virgins
as if you are reaping a royal harvest
for the expense of a simple nod or a grin.

You are now drinking like a country squire
from magical bowl of my hyperbole
that I wouldn't let Apollo or Artemis touch
for the fear of contamination!

MONUMENTS

I don't need to burrow in expensive retreats
to indulge & court my peregrina muse.
I may be anything—a sad griffin,
beleaguered god or gay sailor,
troubled centaur or a shady, always
on the run, immigrant but I can still churn out
monuments from my slipshod basement.

LAST TRYST AT ANN ARBOR CAMPUS

Above the muted whispers of horoscopes
& heavy metal clang of slot machines,
Time is skiing like loons
on its Alpine trajectory.
Your eyes flicker as if waking up
from a gondola dream—
pungent as chives, tinkling like chimes.
Our stares embrace across the table
which is draped in colored squares
of lavender & salmon-red.
We are oblivious to the poor acoustics
& sonic fringe of this Greek bistro
& the sampans of French fries
& the catamarans of Gyros
piled on cheap squatty china
that we both ordered with sub-zero yen.

Our hands freely court.
The soft candles of your knees
singe against mine
& I am getting inebriated.
You are showing off to me
The Sonnets To Orpheus bought at Borders.
We are sipping our Chablis
with panicked abandon.
Your hazel eyes flicker
with echoes of Persian fables.
Your full lips still compete
with Ghalib's ghazals.
A ghost of hibiscus has driven
up its sharp javelins by the pavement
ringed with scarlet gravel.
Lives being drawn in the vortex of traffic.
Hour's fresco looms over
bistro's painted filigree in fading green.
A young woman in a poppy-blue bolero jacket
is swishing by on her cobalt bicycle.
She is smoking a cigarette,
her chignon-gathered hair flame
in a lagoon of blueberry incandescence.

Isn't that sixtyish man
in green slacks & Oxford shirt
with a hint of a goatee & mild Alzheimer's
the Classics professor from Lourdes
who taught us Mallarmé & Proust,
who gave you an A minus
despite your sexy protests
& your bouncy braless blossoms
while I hid my solid A as the cat
hides her excrement
for fear of making you jealous?
The Prof is on his ritual walk
with his Cocker Spaniel.

Five young men in their twenties
breeze by in cool Nikes
parading their hairy wrestler thighs & chests
& Schwarzenegger biceps.
Á flame of gypsy moths rally
under Chinese carnations.
Magpies roughhouse on an ancient elm.
We two are bruised by our knowing
that we both are lying through our teeth
about getting back after you leave the campus.
That we will not go on
being lovers or best friends.

That we will finally bite into
the scythe of Time & bleed out all
memories that once blazed our gaze
& spiked our heartbeats,
that this is the last begrudged weekend
of our fourth year of college,
that all our rendezvous are already spoken for.
That the bay of love is already drying in our hearts.
My memory is already thumbing through
the whispered afterglows
& raw perfumes of our flesh
in the half-lit guest rooms of your dorms
after heavy necking & petting.
I imagine you tonight after the last flowers

of our longing are burnt out & our hearts' guitars
have played their final chords,
you will be frantically packing
bags & suitcases,
checking your cache of shampoos,
gardens of mood altering scents,
my gift of a lilac sari
bordered with sitar & sarod in gold
that I bought you from Leeds
& gifts of other eligible men
that you loved, dated & dared
before I became your
alter shadow & alter echo.

I imagine you tallying your lens cleaners,
blow dryer, shoal of dresses & cheongsams,
cocoons of leggings against an imaginary list.
You complained that parking is too expensive
in downtown Chicago so you are letting me buy your car
at a bargain price. You are leaving by Amtrak
for Chicago tomorrow noon
to share a townhouse with a girlfriend.

A baritone salary & pricy power suits
wait for you at some sky-hugging corporation.
You are going to be their entry level electrical engineer
& I am going to bum around Ann Arbor
for another year to finish up my Poli Sci thesis
& watch a sly time keep gaining amnesiac inches
on the cobwebs of calendars.
I spy the Rosetta stones of your eyes
limned with a gentian blue sadness
as if saying beloved—love must not take hostages—
it should fly unfettered as pelicans,
it should be angle fish light & lucent.
I do want to say yes, yes, beloved & get it over with
& yet my fanatic heart will not let go
the strings of your sunny, mazurka, Meryl Streep
giggling & the sovereign pull of the evenings
that you kindled like a shaman
with your monarch tulip incandescence.

AN ELEGY

Since you took leave I can hardly bear
watching your orphaned garden
but sometimes I linger by it as one might
hang on to an old prayer or love-letter
to quieten my daffodil nerves
& get a grip on my grief & hysteria.

I look at your special rose bush
with a wistfulness that soon
splutters into flush of tears.
I think of the palm-size
blood-roses that never failed
to rivet your attention like a kite catcher.

Those Chianti roses became the markers
of your uncanny gift for periwinkle miracles.
Once a day standing by the deck
you would call out for me to exude & rejoice
how these veils over veils
nymphets had grown bigger
just on a day's spindle, how much more
fringed with fragrance & hora raptures.
Imagine how you would beg me
to stoop before them & inhale their waft
as if they were some new crop of divinities!

I now wonder how you could fall,
with your razor-sharp Iranian smarts,
for those fragile inmates of evanescence
knowing so well how painfully fleeting
are their sepal-smiles, their stingray-bright grins.
Those fawned-over roses of yours
have long been gone—
their anthers, styles, corollas flushed
or gnawed by breeze, rust, mildew & black spots,
their tender hearts tipped over by spring showers
but I can't separate their lost musk
from the perfume of your absence.

The dahlias gleaming in lathered light are still there
looking so strangely familial as though
they have magically absorbed all the hues
of your rainbow deportment
that my heart has gotten used to over the years.
The white dahlias are dressed in the color
of your holier-than-thou daintiness.
The canary-yellow ones are stand-ins
for the tint of your wander-lust
that took us to the Museo del Prado,
Louvre, Borghese gallery & Van Gogh museum.
The bright orange ones are reminders
of your overdrive that finally killed you—
brought you such strumming & jangling angina.

The magenta ones resonate
with the color of your blushing lust
which would sear as my eager lips
probed your gorgeous water lilies.
The russet dahlias sway
as if they are singing of the scarlet strains
of your bloodcurdling jealousies
that almost pushed our marriage
over the abyss half a dozen times.
They proxy as the withering souvenirs
of our hundred breakups
& tear-soaked makeups.

The two peony bushes
that I planted by myself are still
in bloom & self-absorbed like you.
Remember how I had slashed
the underground plastic mantilla
to fill up the exposed underbelly
with fertilizer and dirt.
I always did your bidding
when it came to your garden.
You were the muse of this
ever muddled heaven.

Those long two hours of digging
& dirt pouring to put in the peonies
completely unhinged my daisy back
but I got over the aches & pains
& your slave-driving yen.
I survived to fly back in
to watch the peonies blazing
in the Colorado sun
as if four gallant Persian princes
had just stepped out
of Firdausi's *Book of Kings*
but darling how would I
get over your taking leave
without a phone number
or an address or proper farewell.
Do you think this piety
of babysitting your garden
whose degrees of light,
color tones, slants of greens
you had haggled over
so fiercely with the landscapist,
will make me take its ownership?
Do you really fancy those lavender blue

crocus bulbs, those spangly
deep crimson cistus blossoms
quivering in the opal breeze,
those nervous heart-sick peonies
would ever stare at me as rivetingly
as they gazed at your Diana face?
Lady, are you out of your mind to even think
your garden will slowly cuddle up to me
& kiss off my tears for good
& comfort me like a young lover.
All I can offer your garden
are my services as its guardian angel
while you, you big dance-crazy flirt,
must be dating real cherubs
with hyacinth-grape eyes,
wisteria hands & the electric feet of a tap dancer!

A Masterpiece By Midnight

If you don't grin like dogwoods
listening to my zany
& desultory monologues
& insouciantly watch

how I twist & turn, parry & lunge like breeze
& grow pale by each anguished pause
doing my dream night job of sleeking a poem
like a lapidary,

how I add a seductive line or two
to treat the numb incandescence,

how I bond with the rose-gold celosias
& the trumpet creepers
to augur your midnight bloom.

How I coax the reluctant moon to insinuate
the capricious seasons of your moods.

How I enlist sun's cuddly trombone fingers
to accent the cherry blossom
blush of your vaulted cheeks,

how I groom a derelict evening
to be your courtesan,

how I improvise the lily-blue whimpers
of a tired & tried afternoon
in the smithy of my guts
to make up an Ellington tune.

How I compare the fey
chandeliers of the stars
against the flashing flares
of your lilium-white arms.

How I borrow the hot moons
of your knees, the crepuscular dusk
of your thighs to limn
the fables of aurora borealis.

How I catch the mutterings
of Whitman & Frost
in the liturgy & hymnals
of Bijou traffic.

How I bottle up
in a corolla of a verse
a whole year of loving, wooing,
chasing, teasing,
importunate begging
to your eyes & heart.

How I make a stanza swing
& groove as if
a pubescent ballerina

is baited, dared & swooped
by the trumpets & violins

to dance an iris epiphany
like the first crocus springing

through the snow-fleece
& if I start up early
at the cusp of the evening

then perhaps a lilting masterpiece
will be blooming by midnight.

SHAKESPEARE

I don't care from where
he gets his fabulous cues,
his plot-bouquets like unexpected bounties,
his swooning story lines
like the fandango moves of rose breasted grosbeaks
& the Harlem shakes of a butterfly fish
as long as the soliloquies of his frantic prince,
the lust-hymns of his horny queens
& his treasonous assassin-kings
make my life worth living.
His steel bright, blue wild indigo seas
may be bartered or swiped

from great painters
but not their rubescent outbursts.
His scowling saucy queens
may be the blossoms
of some French brothels,
his hawkish kings
may be little runts or cheap models
from Denmark or highlands of Scotland
but not their golden bales of broodings.

Exhilarating & stirring in our soul's
buoys & clinking clearings
Shakes-master is our raging manhood,
our pulsating dawn, our hushed gloaming
against the dark pines & black alders
in a cloudburst of kestrels & herring gulls.

He is our Rembrandt, our Peter Paul Rubens
for all seasons & hours & bi-polar swings.
He is our jostling light over the strapping
cypresses of emerald-green infinities,
our lucky viola virtuoso against Apollo's
splendid harp playing!

A Journalist's Travelogue

I have seen the willows dance the swell Macarena & virgins
break their chastity vows under their gilt canopies,

I have spied God's violet sage hands
playing harp on metallic winds.

I have caught red maples' swoon & quiver,
heard pomegranate trees whisper & muse
with supernal wisdom.

I have seen pluming angels rise from factory chimneys
in Michigan's frost-nipped dawns.

I have seen a SUV toss & turn
on a twister's tongue, hogs flying up like corks
from the shaft of a barn in Arkansas.

I have seen Mahatmas & great saints
being sucked in like beetles & moths
in history's vortex.

I have shared pillows & pleasantries
with call-girls fit to be queens
in brothels of Lahore & Bangkok.

I have haggled with pimps & hoodlums
as gracious as Pope John Paul & Dalai Lama,
seen death playing Mahjong
on streets of Beijing & Bombay.

I have heard a Serb zealot on tape
ordering a Muslim son to rape
his mother's body just stilled but warm
by a blast of gunshot.

Believe me, my good friend, that is more
than what most mortals know or dream
or trade or take in a whole lifetime.

The Tutor

I trained you so superbly, so elegantly
like a tutor to a suicide bomber,
how to be doggedly focused
& infinitely distant, how to be an alpha bitch,
how to act as if there is no difference
between the tabooed & the good.
I made love to you the very glum evening
my mother was laid to rest.
Was it because the rubbing act reflected
the sudden trauma of a man freshly orphaned
that now both his parents rudely taken
by the saber hands of death
he must pretend as if he is not intimidated?

I vividly remember after
the macabre hemorrhage
of the sexual crest I wept
like a young Chechen widow
& the downpour was so thunderous
that you became distraught
& you too started to wail & whimper.

Twenty years have passed
when I tutored you how to tango
with a rank sacrilege
with your treasonous eyes,
devil-may-care yoni & flashy breasts.
I am now finally pinned & grounded
by a protracted & picturesque death
& you preen and prance around my lurid bed
& bring new lovers home to cast spells
& they kiss & undress you & wash you
with their semen & sweat in front of my clear view
while I beg for a glass of wine or a sip of whisky
& you smilingly serve me up with the same
seedy insolence & defiant pertness
that I helped you so diligently perfect
that no in-session death should crave,
that no cancerous cells should caress,
that no festering brain should cradle!

WHEN I DIE

When I die, beloved, nothing will change
to mark or mourn my exit.

The sun will not be blotted out
by the dust-storm of my death.

The killer housecat wouldn't take a sabbatical
from her hunting & skinning
of baby rabbits & bird nestlings
even for few days,

the blue-bouffant skies will carry on
with their parlor games of smokes
& mirrors & baroque sound bites
showing off their sumptuous bracelets

& earrings in summer & spring.
The deers & opossums will
keep hitching themselves
around the blasé rims of SUVs
& trailers on rural highways.

Moon's brazen striptease
will go on with no fanfare.

The amber light as usual will nervously paint
the scalloped darkness
in bursts & squiggles & plasma veins
as if on Meth or crack cocaine.

The stars' hieroglyphics will show
no scars or stains of the vanished flowers
of my tempers or melancholy.

The begonia breeze will not skip a beat.
Iced up bushes like painted eyes
will light up with casements of emerald chokers.

The braided Rastafarian waters
of Niagara Falls by heft of habit
will sluice down with their tiaras
of onyx & diamonds.

The streets of Detroit will go on
bristling with winter's havocs & deep freeze
& the parks will put on gleamy skirts
of icebergs for children's pleasure.
The summers when summoned
will toot their horns with violet irises,
orange poppies & goldenrods.
The storksbills will continue to stun
with their fuchsia helter tops.

But only you, beloved, will embrace
the lavender rhododendrons of grief
& you will hunch over to read the clutch
of my letter-poems over & over
as if to squeeze out their exquisite poisons;
then you will proceed to burn them
by the same beer garden in Munich
where we stole moments of respite from walking
the Deutsch Museum to blend
our young & middle-aged wines & lips.

Perhaps, you will save the curled ashes
of my letters in a mega-envelope
to be spread by Seine or Rhine or both.
In four to six months you will get your grooves back.
After the last lumps of needless regrets & cowry tears
you will demurely pick up a young lover
at the Whitney or Guggenheim
or at a jazz club rasping with saxophones,
trumpets, bass & trombones.
This time no hustler, no swindler of frantic words.
In Cassandra Wilson's husky voice
& sleek armeria-red laughter, you will present
your two golden retrievers to your new lover
by telling him: "over there is Oliver—just Oliver
—no Oliver Twist or Oliver North—at least not yet
over here is Striker never stricken or struck out"

& an estrus-blushed grin will emblazon your face.

PEACOCK'S DANCE

Sharon—You told me—
there would be sheaves of time
after the party for catmint nuzzling
& for brushing my pent up lips
against your larkspur cleavage
& to undo your headstrong seagulls
burning your tight burgundy sweater.
There will be time to refresh
the coral lipstick & the purple eye shadows
& to align the scarlet-flax evening
& it's violet eye-linings
with the persimmon diction of our yearnings.
There will be time for me to be ravished
by the Corinthian splendor of your legs
& for the insurgency of lust to blossom
like a bush of lilacs & for the cherry red
smooching & nipping in the rosewood kitchen.

There will be time after we have prayed
for compassion & clemency
for the frost bitten junipers, asters & clematis
& for the big spruce naked
& stripped down as menorah.
There will be time after old pickup lines
are overspent with unintended slurs
& the beer cans are picked & expensive China
has been rinsed for the dishwasher
& smoked salmon & Greek salad
& hearts of braised artichokes, pickled octopi,
skewered shrimps & peppers
are put away in the birch white frig
& Jane's debonair drool is wiped clean
from the Tree of life on our Persian rug
after her incredible sax playing.

There will be time before
the night is nibbled & cannibalized
by the campus pundits & hard-core
cabalists of doom & apocalypse.

There will be time after flag wavings
of our ravenous Methuselah aches & pains
& the brazen rituals of blaming our trespasses,
our stutterings & memory lapses
on God, Freud, Marx & Lenin
& pinning of our shortcomings
on our hard-drinking truck-driving dads
& on our mace carrying postal moms.
There will be time after we have paid the devil
his proper dues for all our three-penny
triumphs & winnings
& florid valedictorian speeches
that we can no longer lampoon,
recite or turn into flashy jingles.

There will be time after the booze has brought
the bronze nipples of every trite proverb
& aphorism to an absolute frenzy.
There will be time after the dredging
of Fahrenheit moments
in the vermilion barn of our memories
for history's rumor mills & gossip books.
There will be time after we have shown off
our lacerating laser brilliance
& flash-flooding wit
& have asked silly arse questions such as:
"Why it is freezing when an arboreal moon
is glowing like yellow daisies?"

There will be time after we have shown off
our seraphic credentials & pins & dubious links
to Rimbaud & Caravaggio with impish grins.
There will be time after we have swaggered
that we have the power to magnetize & mesmerize,
that we don't need Krishna's blessings
to write our own *Wasteland* & *King Lear*.
There will be time after all
the pimping & whoring of language
is played out by Modern Arts
& linguistics professors high on orange bitters,
faintly stoned on dense malt of Guinness.

There will be time after all the ogling
& self-teasing & breast grading
of the well-vaulted, well-decked
geishas of your Econ 507 class
by the horny overweight dean of Arts & Science.
There will be time after we have lived
& died & dissipated in the chinks
& interludes of vicious put downs
camouflaged as innocent quips.
There will be time after all the half-drunk,
half-amorous hearts have been
sent home giggling & grinning,
dank in their armpits & underpants
& good-byes are hurled & hung on the frigid air
& porch lights have been dismissed

for the raw ballads of the cicadas & the crickets
& our patient cats & labradors
have been fed & sent to their basement bunkers
& curtains are drawn hurriedly
to lend ourselves to the verities of flesh.
There will be time to retire the panhandling wind
blaspheming against the windowpanes
& to inflame my limping middle-aged amphibian
by your steamy Southern Comfort kiss.
There will be time to savor
the alchemy & enigma of silence
& let the fingers & tongues do all
the talking, sparring, groping & grazing.

There will be time to take you
to the tall bedroom mirror
& swoon in your adagio undressing
& feel the world is still a supple tangerine
in the palms of my hands.

Sharon: my kitchen goddess,
my closet harlot,
my pillow deity, my soul-sibling
that time is ripe like a scarlet apricot.

THE RECKONING HOUR

Where did all those giddying years swish by
when we soaked up in a tub of blue vertigo
waiting to team up with Paul Verlaine
& Victor Hugo?

The splash of those frenzied years
dripping as slashed wrists seems as spooky
as the sudden gash of un-latched breeze
just before we enter a shadowy chamber
redolent with the passing of a beloved
& fresh moss roses. The wallop of sudden chill,
the eerie Braille of gestures,
the hushed tensions of that haloed air
are achingly reminisced many years later.
Now in the twilight hours of a life
not completely botched or redeemed,
I wonder if we did buy the best frankincense
to offer life the apt accolade.
Did our poetic lines held enough razzmatazz
& voltage as keel-billed toucan?
If our blasting laughter was buoyant enough
to lift all the doleful village-hearts?

If our ballads had enough pull & charisma
to rivet the blue jays
cruising towards a poppy red sunset?
If all our crystal tumblers & Russian chalices
were filled with sparkling wines
& raspberry raptures?
Did we really overreach
our talents' balconies & bell towers?
Did we hasten to offer our alohas
to a grand but reticent talent
pretty as rainbow lorikeets
or we were too frantic peddling
our own shoddy Tupperware?
Did we burn enough night oil to deserve
this bluebird breeze, that dusk-red surf,
that hushed grove rustling with gilded

aspens & flowering cherries,
that tout kerchief of blue morphos
& kites of ocher lacewings,
for those crazy isles in the clabbered skies
puzzling the grosbeaks,
those heather-cloaked hills floating
on the candle-holders of blue-gilled mists?
Were we beholden enough for our sweet children
dizzy with dance & albatross brilliance?
Did our eyes swam in diamonds
watching the blazing gifts
of potentillas & flag-irises
or when we saw the white hot egrets
dreaming they were trumpet lilies?

Did we bow our heads in thanks
for the spinning fireworks of stars,
for that slinking moon who wasn't
a spy at all but a sweet goofball?
Did we do our best or did we just
slouch & glide on borrowed grace
to rake in the radiance?
In our life's dusk-tinged gloom,
we will have some scarlet regrets.
That we should have hustled harder
to become well-groomed in Borge & Heidegger.
That we didn't ache enough for a Brazilian
heartthrob who spoke in tottering Hebrew.

That our gaze should have perched longer
on a wimpled lake or a fading fresco.
That we should have read a lot more in a half-smile
or a desperate embrace. That one should have phoned
more often one's vanishing maman even though
she had ceased to be the darling soul
one had vastly adored like a bush of foxgloves;
but what if the patina of guilt is dense as ferns.
What purgatory will we seek then in a sudden
spike of panic, in those evenings of dwindling,
tapered off candles & spluttering hopes?

A Warning

Man, your have become a big-time wino
wearing your cirrhosis & vertigo
like a Star of David.

You can hardly eat because your liver is smelting.
Look at your velour waist, your tulle torso.
You have shrunk to the weight
of a scraggy ten-year-old boy & a famished husky.
You used to have Leo DiCaprio's draw & charisma
& a ready regatta of spiky bee bam jokes.
You had loved fly-fishing since your early teens.
You were always chasing & courting
rainbow trouts in wide riffles, meanders,
pocket waters, short rapids.
You had awesome stamina.
You slayed *Remembrance Of Things Past*
in 2 harrowing, coffee-rimmed weeks.

I was so taken by your daunting feat
& now look at you, wasting away & crumbling
like a dead silver mine.
When you can't down a vodka
you shake like taro leaves.
Your feet have started to swell
as if you ford daily in a lake
bristling with deadly chemicals.
So what if your wife died of a horrid
breast cancer? That is fourteen months past.
You don't owe her a similar *La Bohème* departure.

You have grieved enough, my brother,
& the family has suffered profusely.
Please, please don't cry like sculptures.
Spare me your martyr's tears. Listen, I am
single & have no widow to leave behind.
I can no longer watch you waft towards Hells' pavilions.
If you don't come with me to register
at the rehab center, I will end up
shooting you & myself with daddy's gun.

IN PRAISE OF GAIETY

Poetry is the only hotel lounge
where I can be a perfect libertine & weep
for my ex-lovers & un-requited loves
without breaking my wedding vows
or can have repast with Sophocles & Cervantes
without fretting about the proper dress code
& the three-figure dinner bill.

Poetry is the redoubt of my madcap freedoms,
fecund as the rainforests of dreams,
numinously scented & hushed as séances.

To me it is my mother's sluicing milk
filled with magic nutrients & anti-oxidants.

In my Gatling gun cantos
I am Richard the Lion Hearted
marching towards Jerusalem
to feud the swarthy, charismatic heathens
& dizzying Arabian temps.

I am Jacob wrestling with the Angel of Death.

I am Job cursing God's aqua marine arse.

I am Spinoza soliciting men to get drunk
on a love-less God.

I am Don Quixote being taken
to the shed by Sancho Panza.

I am Madame Bovary mixing rat poison
with ice cream for my sea lavender apotheosis.

I am Prince Hamlet—the troubled teen
from Denmark debating with my father's ghost.

I am King Lear grieving
with the temperamental Fool
for my daughters' avarice & rampant capitalism.

I am Garcia Lorca stumbling
as a giant deep damask-rose
under the bullets' canopy.

I am Che Guevara wasting away & waiting
in the gloom of Argentinean jungle
for the Fascist soldiers & the Prima Dona of death.

I am Maria Callas begging my agent to let me sing
Carmen in my battered, lack-luster voice.

I am Gerard de Nerval finally ready
to hang myself with bat like alacrity.

I am Fidel Castro taunting an arrogant,
unforgiving Roman empire.

In poetry's opalesque lakes I swim & wade
with the butterfly-lipped screen naiads
like Angelina Jolie, romp with every
Playboy centerfold that Donald Trump
could buy & trade on E-Bay.

In my poetry's Sierra mountains I am Solomon's commandant,
I am Christ's perfidious & smooching sidekick.

I am Aristotle's luminous ghost
leading a Type A Macedonian king.

I am Louis Armstrong's fire cracking trumpet
blazing the Mississippi's waters,

I am Charlie Parker's flaming tenor sax
with a rapt God in the audience—
So don't hold me back you envywarts,
you self-serving shrinks. Learn to soak yourself
in my gaiety's ravishing gale
& be grateful like a Magi King!

KARACHI

You were once a city of celosias, hibiscus & jasmines,
a city of contested incandescence with Lahore.
In your desert margins, the flames of echinocactus
with vermilion blossoms were eye candies
for our summer-lapped eyes.

You flapped like posse of red-wattled
lap-wings & mustard-tinged coppersmiths.
You chugged, you bellowed, you steamed
as your exuberant poets like Josh & Faiz.

You only flaunted few purple-jacaranda
& sheesham trees to comfort our scalded eyes.
The sob & boom of your streets
like a hundred thundering metal drums
kept us alert & jolted

but you had no fan tailing belfry-towers,
no baroque palaces with straggling gardens,
no crystal-flamed opera houses
or feet-swelling museums
to justify your strand into history's hazel braids

& yet your emerald shores
courted by the soughing Arabian Sea, your nervous
blue-sage heavens & humped low-hills,
worsted, gecko-gray, sun-buffed
like hunched gypsies
over their steaming teakettles
were good enough to tug my Tom Sawyer heart

& fill my eyes with hot pearls.
Oh! the city of my first blistering love,
my tusk-bright dahlia teens,
my dark-red mahogany youth.

Your plazas once embroidered
with belladonna lilies, turmeric-tinted
sunflowers, wild lilacs, gardenias & mums
are now flecked with smelly dopies—

snorting & dispensing poison
spreading like spiny thorn tree.
Your turreted mosques that once crescendoed
with slumber-slashing muezzins' calls
are now freesia-red with Shiite blood.

Oh! city of million scary contours & blurs,
I no longer bawl for your woes, twitches, jitters,
for your slashed wrists bleeding with hemp,
your tear-gassed streets, malls, berms,
dreary tenements & bedraggled kiosks
& parks sowing despair & bitterness.

I no longer grieve for your
garbage-rimmed pavements festering
with human & animal sediments.
Just thirty years past
I felt so safe & salubrious
in your ululating tabernacle breasts.

Your major boulevards
were always sleepless.
The opium-laced-tea houses
were my favorite haunts
where buddies fleshed out ideas,
smuggled news, cigarettes,
bragged about humping lush girlfriends
& lampooned the beer-bellied general

naming himself the president
& his whisky sipping plump mistresses.
Remember how your minstrel
salmon-flipping sea
for some ten years served as my
lone confessional in the evenings.

That sea now retches not with just dead
weeds, remains of sea urchins
& sand tasseled condoms,
but is heavy with chemicals
& technicolor grease.

The brackish waters swelled up
my feet every time I bared them
to receive the proverbial baptism
& now your acquired taste for mayhem
& shoddy martyrdom from Talibans

leaves me just beer-chilled, you creep.
Bards like Faiz, Josh, Shakir
are now all nimbused & draped
in immortality's dyes & daffodils—

then from whom could I have received
approving nods or mute disdains
or looks of mild shock & bewilderment
for my topiary of topaz verses?

I am disgusted by your scaly sights
when I see men getting robbed & hurt
in shambolic midday traffic
while nobody stops or bothers or frets
& police only cater to the affluent victims.
I will never return to you again.

Don't let your gorge rise because
I let go your hand & sauntered off
to a generous & safer land.

What would I have reaped if I had stayed
in your jangling embrace,
my city of toxic grails
but to kill with relish or get slaughtered
by a Sunni fanatic like a sacrificial goat.

Have you ever thought of that
ochre-whirled outcome?

You jealous resentful caterwauling whore.
You dreadful charas-glutted
world-class eyesore!

FOR MY FIRST LOVE

Thirty-two years are too long,
too woozy, too surreal, too tempest-tossed
to go back to trace your deep-scarlet
hyacinth scent in a country
that I left three coup d'etats ago,
whose roadmaps, plazas, shopping malls,
coconut-white minarets & foam-wept shorelines
have been so rashly reworked or razed
by the entropy of tyranny & time
that they completely confound me
on each visit every dozen years.

But if I could ever find you braiding
your granddaughter's curls
for Sunday school sitting
next to an archway of sweetbrier roses,
or resting by yourself on a sofa chair
peering over a summer garden
blazing with palm beachbells, purple
banana blossoms, star-apples, Himalayan
maples, mango & Chiku trees,

how could I ever reveal
by what ruses & fancy's arabesques
that while leaving Karachi
I could never suspect
that your sea lavender face
would so itch itself
in my memory's palms,
that your dreams like
tousled stars will keep ticking
like clock alarms
that I would never manage to turn off
& snuff out your memories-candles
in my synapses.

That your pretty cinnamon ocelot eyes
as big as figs would follow me
like an unrelenting muse like Marx,
like Freud, like God, like death?

MORNING AFTER A MINOR ANGINA

A night like black tar heroin has just left
like a reluctant bull
to continue its steady advance & mayhems.
A peach blossom moon still lurks & clomps
like a weak & weary argument.
The wind warily dances
over the thick-matted, slabbered grass.
My heart flutters as a fretful quail.
I am a little fatigued & anxious but no sweat.

So go tell the ruby-necklaced humming bird,
the pink Aloha climbers, the tallits of musk roses,
the sour apples that are the understudy
for crocus corms,
the steepled blue pines, the junipers,
the apple groves with ruby earrings,
the silver-ribboned pussy willows,
the pair of loquacious cardinals,
the rabble of rowdy magpies,
the whirring thong of half dozen blue jays;

put on early notice
the cawing rooks in ebony buntings,
the bashful breeze dragging its feet
behind the silver maples,
the fragrant tarragon herbs,
the crimson peppers, the swirl of cilantro stalks,
the sprawling mints, the absinthe-green tomato teats,
the slack-breasted zucchinis, the armadillo gourds.

Also telepath sun's golden albatross,
the still groggy lily-white mountains
& the papaya-hued school bus
with whimpering half-sleepy
elementary school towhees & warblers.
Tell them I am no longer grounded,
that I am ready to come out
to play tag or hide-n-seek or charades
or burst in an evensong or ditty
like a purple sunbird.

PORTRAIT OF A POET IN HIS TEENS

Even though he was a lanky teen in cowlicks
we knew that secretly he pined
for Brando's forceps, if not for his
clipped, minced, high falsetto voice;
yet his soft gladiola arms never lost
their girlish suppleness
but whenever his gaze ambled
a sun-drenched dove-gray pavement
he would exude: "I see a pall of
quicksilver-sheened catbird-clouds."

The fruited quince trees in the orchards
were for him light-green brides
on palanquins in a Chinese pastoral play.
He truly fancied that every cheerleader
in the high school gym
was fitted with oleander, brimful, bobbling
boobs & their lute buttocks were
as handsome as Georgia O'Keeffe's lotuses,

that their kisses, if he ever snagged one,
had to be Baklava-sweet, strawberry-tangy,
but it was his penchant for Laelia orchid miracles
which made us think that if he ever saw a pair
of lovely bare breasts in some careless
window or swimming pool or on a brazen surfer
he would simply pass out
from the awesome epiphany
& when he was jeered & teased
for the madness of his
high-wire embellishments
he would simply quip:
"Man, I am in the business
of mango tight raptures.
You protest too much?"

We chuckled often about
his prayer rugs of metaphors.
Once he told us:

"Poetry is like a vicious carol snake
that I sleep with every Lolita evening
& one day for sure it will lick me dead
but till then I will gladly eat
her jasper-green eggs."
We wished to tell him
that his Shelley-swept,
Rimbaud-stung seashell eyes
were blood-streaked with eternity's quills
but we never dared
although we hardly doubted
that he could snare, if he wanted,
moon's zinc-glazed tambourine,

sun's passion flower
or cloisonné butterflies of galaxies
by his ball pen's often bruised,
crossed, curlicued, gutted phrases
& we often prayed that someday
he would be handed the magic wand
to turn a cattleya orchid to a jelly fish,
a jellyfish to a mandarin newt

and then the newt back to an orchid;
we all understood that this great
metamorphosis was worth our wait
but he was killed in a few months
by an impatient leukemia at age sixteen
& we still can't fathom
why he is ten feet under
& we are still afloat & airborne!

THE PRENUPTIAL COVENANT

You are no Simone de Beauvoir
& I am no John Paul Sartre.
Let's make it blazingly crystal
as Colorado's pimpernel skies
that under no earthly or heavenly alibis
you will have any paramours
even if your are bereft in Peruvian jungles
writing a romantica novel
& likewise I will have no clueless groupies
splashing in our bathtub
when you are yawningly
signing your fiction books on an East-coast
to West-coast whirlwind book tour.

We may not ever get hitched
& pelted with basmati rice pearls
& crimson ululations that Middle Easterns
hurl with such gusto & verve
but we will share the same shed & shelter
& lolling twin bed & do *Bolero*

four times a week making
exceptions for splitting headaches
due to mounting job-stresses
or depression stirred by writer's block
or inevitable kitchen skirmishes
with our finicky, make believe mother-in-laws.

In slippery moments of high tide quietus
we will not stain each other's ears
by the names of our ex-lovers
& then blame it on lousy light,
in-attention, rush of Tequilas or Viagra.

I will continue to dazzle & seduce you
with my high-end Mogul cuisine
& will begrudgingly take on
house cleaning & writing of bills
& you will immerse yourself in house chores

like painting, plumbing & gardening
which I guess aren't that sweat-bearing.
I hope you will agree.

We will not read each other's works
& then insist on revisions & second drafts
but we will insinuate & suggest authors
of high voltage eminence
who can't be ignored or trifled with.

We will only get tipsy on Merlot
& cheap rosé and occasionally
we will allow ourselves long decanters
of blue Margaritas on hot prickly
summer noons.

You will have the picking rights
for all the art works & house flowers
& yes, you can keep your two geriatric cats
as perennial houseguests,
but we will have no dogs whatsoever—
no beagles, no dachshunds, no golden retrievers.

I will show maximum forbearance
for your unconditional love for Kafka,
honey-baked Yani & that rank surrealist Miro
but you will never ever bring up
Emily Dickinsen or Borge or Celan
or the wild antics of your lesbian shrink.
I just hope I haven't given up too much
that I will come back to regret.
If you find this covenant genial, equitable
immensely doable & cathartic
& not at all life threatening,
gender-bending or insidiously partisan
say or hum "agreed" & sign it
with a huge French kiss
& by taking off your deep-plunged,
black-laced wonder bra.

BALZAC RISING

I am both Bonaparte & Lord Nelson
in the Waterloo of letters.
I am short, squat, stubby-nosed,
fat-arsed but the whole
rough-and-tumble universe grants
that I am a tireless colossus.
I am a fire storm, a twister's eye,
a blizzard of bristling butterflies,

a rumbling smithy of white hot iron,
a fretwork of fulminating bones & terrors,
a blitz of snaking blood
& going strong on twenty two cups
of strong Hawaiian Kona coffee.
God Almighty, I know with your infinite patience
of a black red-necked stork

you would love to crack my lungfish skull
squelching my famous hubris-soaked head
that will be displayed someday
in Muse Renoir forever,
& yes, I will someday be humbled
& would become a playpen for the ambitious dust,
a trampoline for disgusting bugs but till then,
God dearest, I will dance the cake walk, the jerk,
the conga, the watusi, the swing & sing & swagger
& wear my sequined cowboy boots
& show off my dapper ivory-gold staff
to all gawkers around the Champs-Elysées,

I will flirt & make love
to every cute concierge,
chambermaid, waitress, flower girl
& groupie across the two continents.

Make comrades out of Saturn, Mars, Jupiter,
make friends with Mark Twain & Henry James,
get drunk on sun's crimson rum
& sip the finest lagers & cognacs

& speak my mind & aerate
my over-worked acrobat heart
& be an electric drill in Apollo's guts.

I will be the font of envy for Victor Hugo,
Dumas & Sainte-Beuve
who will someday be my pallbearers.
I will filch from Sophocles & Shakespeare,
from Parisian pimps, tart hookers,
terminal gamblers,

from the hustlers, the gigolos,
the jugglers, the idlers,
the smugglers, from that trickster
& jinxed Odysseus.
I will plagiarize lines from shyster
lawyers, shopkeepers,
janitors, grifters, bartenders, drug dealers,
noblemen & their snobbish
butlers & gardeners,

I will liaise with irises, tulips,
anthuriums, lilacs
& all the known splendors
that are planted & flaunted
to shame the over-proud angels.

I will lift phrases from sport writers,
senators, talking heads & skid row bums
to take home what was always mine,
to glean my own majestic colognes,
my own hallmark brews,
my own divine comedies

& I will keep tearing off pages
after pages from the book of life
& God of Israel & Palestine, I will
rewrite & improvise your unsavory,
tedious, impossible manuscript
till my last sweltering breath!

IF YOU KNEW MY IMPERFECTIONS

If you knew my imperfections, my fault-lines,
you would have balked twice before accepting
a joy ride to Clifton Beach
where we eavesdropped
on the breathless Bhangra of the waves
& spied on the moon rolling,
like a mountain lion
smudging his taffeta singlet

against the debris of old beer cans, wine bottles
& the crossberry-white diapers
while we kissed & hugged & held hands
till the jealous beach guard asked us to leave
to spare the innocent teenagers
from the Mae West fonts of our lewdness.

You would have spared yourself
early enough if you knew
what a superb cad I was in the making
& how when we met
your best friend from college
at Somerset Mall while she sipped
on the frothy Caramel Macchiato
I secretly pined to devour
her perfectly cleavaged
scorpion-stung, pillow cased
Scarlett Johansson's lips
& caress her pergola of damask roses.
My slut-eyes couldn't have masked
my indecent yearnings.

Beloved, you wouldn't have touched me
with a ten yard pole if you had really known
how I almost convinced
with Iago's cunning & persistence
the beautiful Lebanese sophomore
we hosted last spring to pose in nude for me
but it didn't come to pass because
I lacked the courage of my convictions

& a good camera with film
while you fanatically shopped
for my parents' 50th wedding anniversary.

You would have held back
your indulgent applause
for my poem denouncing Hafiz and Paz
if you knew it was the first step
to a bittersweet trajectory
that our alliance would became over time.
If you knew my radiant flaws
as the hoop-skirted clouds know the blemishes
of the philandering moon
you wouldn't have fancied me
for no more than an afternoon.

If you knew how vastly useless, colorblind
to spatial kinships & maladroit I truly was
you wouldn't have placed me above
your exquisite wardrobe, your French perfumes,
& your potbellied Elephant God.

If you knew how my memory was shot
& feckless like my roving bowie knife eyes
& knew about my readiness to forget
the phone numbers & shopping lists
as soon as they were delivered or flashed
you would have taken more kindly
the good consul of your wise aunt
& restrained the mare of your deluded heart.

Yet I have suspected all along
that you knew all this for the longest time
almost from the first date & the first slush kiss
& yet you have loved me nonetheless
despite my spotted-lilium impieties.
& I have nothing to offer you
but a whale-size thank you
for your stubborn recklessness
for taking me back each week as the pinewoods
hug the faithless fog as the apple grove
suckles eternally the Spanish moss.

HERR SCHILLER

I first met her in a skimpy,
T-shaped teahouse in Leeds
with an ambling luster-rich moon
balancing himself on the crutches
of a redwood tree like a sloshed skinhead.

We both were students then.
I was a Paki Maoist, she was Franco-German
with no radical views on politics,
her papa was a well-heeled
diplomat posted in Beijing.
She was a gorgeous high-cheek-boned girl,
her curves caused me to glower & fight often
with a stiletto-glare against the leering stares
of men in restaurants, omnibuses, subways, parks.

Her swiveling hips stirred me more
than the flapping wings of the stars
or the thistles & the buttercups
in bloom that summer of our raptures.

Her ears were softer than walnuts' lobes.
She adored Schubert & Viennese pastries,
She worshipped Picasso & Chagall,
& I naturally adored every big or tiny miracle
that she was smitten with.

We will call each other silly names.
I will call her my dear Greta Garbo
even though she had never seen her films
& she would call me Herr Schiller
whose works I had not yet read,
splayed or skinned.

We lived in small dorm rooms
which didn't get much of sun's gilded Mojito.
We mostly met in public parks & watched
the showy acrobatics of lapwings
except when we wanted to get horizontal
on our stormy beds.

I will play with her soft opalesque hands
accented with pink under the shadowy slats
of auburn hawthorns, billowed lindens,
flowering golden rain & weeping willows
while trees hovered, whispered
& swung in place like rows upon rows
of inverted violas & cellos,
evening sun with his ruddy grace
courted my Greta as fiercely as I did.

I no longer remember if her kisses were
sweeter than gingerbread cakes
tinged with cinnamon & molasses
or if they were as divine as coconut flecked
almond truffles freshly baked
but I remember vividly
that each kiss did improve each wine sip.

Sometimes it seemed that lucky old sun
had nothing to do but caress
& accent her Bavarian high cheeks
& to make me superbly jealous.
She would bring the baguettes & the Swiss cheese
& I would fetch the cheap French wines.

I could never get enough of her grass pea eyes
even though her calyxed mouth
with all its sweet vividness
competed with her eyes endlessly like a sibling
or like Zivi Zhang against Gong Li
in *Memoirs of a Geisha.*

I would kiss the rose buds of her eyes
that reflected so tenderly the long-sleeved
moonbeams & the blue shimmer of the lake.
Her thighs were always warm under
her checkered skirts.
Her raptures chewed up so much of my time
that I almost failed my final term.

I would read my imperfect, callow poems to her
& she would just grin softly & wouldn't raise
a critical eyebrow as if she expected me
to master poetic diction
as I had mastered her charms' lexicon.
Three months later she left the campus abruptly
to nurse her ailing father.

She departed with kiss-laced vows
that she would write often & visit soon.
I now realize how flawed I was in trusting
the eloquent hours, the suave reassuring moon,
the deep shadows of the sycamores,
lindens & goldenrains & her tremolo embraces.

My "Greta" so I hear,
is now an English Lit. Prof in Leipzig,
happily married to a low-brow
Indian cardiologist
who has full dominion over her courtly beauty.
He is an unassuming, quiet man
who knows nothing
about the spurious gallantry of words,

about the anguished foreclosures of love,
about poetry's ersatz stupors
& three penny epiphanies,
its phony incantations,
its cheap frizzles, frills, flounces, fangles,
its spectacular delusions & enticements,

its heaping letdowns
like the felled cypress in the park
I came upon in Leeds that summer evening
when I kissed her last.

THE FOG

It turns the clotted-cream sky
into a ghost town.
No dikes, no riverbanks,
no thundering waterfalls
can slow down its temperamental armies.

Fog—the accidental tourist takes over
hectors of maize crops, rumbling airports,
rows of tobacco farms & cotton fields
& seals its claims to baritone
shipyards, fairgrounds,
narcoleptic bridges, phallic swash of towers
& watch with smug satisfaction
boroughs after boroughs,
precincts after precincts
stoically submit to its ivory mandate.

The fog lays its boot camps over the soccer fields,
over the convention hall draped in glass.
It wraps its skein of churned white yoke
over creation's eyes to muddle up twirling
geometries, contoured tendons,
nuanced arteries of things into a chaos
of primeval winds & stellar dust

as if it is reshuffling, re-sorting
unwieldy deck of creation
till all cards become hoary phantom fishes
in its spindly aquarium.
Notations of space lose their key markers,
shaggy curves slurp sharp tangents,
circles collapse into elliptical morels.

Fog's imperial reign remains
unchallenged, unraveled, un-protested
until the sun wakes up & orders
his golden paratroopers,
sky walkers, sierra rangers for invasion
& only then very painstakingly
the task of land reclaiming commences.

The inebriated fog stumbles, flounders
through its cowardly retreat
like the Napoleon's infantry
winnowed by Russian winters.
Elms, birches, red maples are re-born
with their spiny inevitable splendor.
Buildings begin to sleek their glassy curves,
& gloat again on their staggering musculature.
Bridges show off their sharp elbows, ridge works,
painted sparkling ribs.

In celebration of freedom
cars crackle with infectious mirth,
trucks dance their vulgar bomba,
the opera house soars in full opulence
as if Evita has mutated into Madonna's flesh,
the church bells flaunt & lift
their metallic bra-less breasts
& becoming resumes
a flashy ménage à trois
with time & memory.

FREEDOM

He had endured exquisite afflictions,
the crowning one was love—
He was ever chasing tenderness
as a lad chasing kites & rabbits
though the most vexing one
of his afflictions was God
as if the divine grace could whittle
the tears & thorns of loneliness.

Well, tenacity of impotence
& neighborhood of death
relieved him of both burdens.

Now he could fly anywhere
that he desired—
to vegetate or ruminate
on the wings of his
turbo-charged skylark fancy.

THINKING OF YEATS

I know, Mrs. Robinson, a poem is not a talisman
or a soft-touch voodoo doll.
I can't prick its cheek or twist its arms
to make you wince or flick
or churn with anguish.
It can't prompt you to say "Oh yes, your are on,"
& I am not some suburban shaman
to cure you from your bourgeois hang-ups.
I know a poem's dismal amplitude
and miasmic range.
I don't presume at all that at the end of this reading
with only sixteen souls in the audience,
including a snoring toddler
& a fretful Great Pyrenees,
you will come up to me & whisper
"I am yours for the taking—at least for the evening."

A poem is a wistful specter, a luminous phantom
of a soul in crimson agony
waddling in manic-depressive swamps.
It is not the swing vote to change a man's chances
to get closer to a woman's heart or crotch.
Even a Nobel couldn't persuade Maud to wed Yeats.
It couldn't bridge the metaphysical leagues
between Beatrice & Dante.
For sure you will get up & flash your sweet
& harried thank-you with a tiara of a smile worthy
of Keats's lapis incandescence

& then you will quickly leave the room
to small talk, panic, despair, half-empty Cabernet bottles,
cheese & crackers & halved strudels
to rush back to your comforting home
to grade all those lit term papers
lounging on your couch & dining table
& then you will glide into your husband's
superbly sculpted Rambo arms
& perhaps think of the fatuous pathos
of my not so mango-tight, not so compelling verses
& smile faintly with a sliver of melancholy.

WAS IT WORTH IT?

Sometimes I wonder if it was worth it
having missed out on my two sisters' flowering
into violet-sage womanhood,
most of all their beautiful mezzo-soprano voices
that I only got to be friends with
when they smuggled them to the United States
& were already wading into their thirties.

Was it worth it to lose out on
their laughter's wallop of twenty years
& not regaling all those offerings
for some dubious & secondhand pleasures?

Was it worth it leaving them all alone
to fend for themselves
without a male protector
after my daddy's death
& let them be bothered daily
by the third world snake pit thugs & goons

while I relaxed with Genet & Gin-o-tonic,
& sang along with Fats Waller's *Honeysuckle Rose*,
& inflamed my gaze with Ingres's *Odalisque*
& Klimt's gold-bosomed goddesses
& courted films of Kurosawa & Fellini
& dug my heels into Van Morrison & Bob Dylan.

Was it fair to delude myself as if I were some
fledgling Gauguin leaving for the South Seas
to court a sultry Jessica Alba destiny
& enjoy my share of debauchery not knowing
in the new country I would always live
under the dangling saber of shame which fell
over me a dozen times whenever
my albino bosses figured
that I was no longer sleek & thoroughbred
to hoof around in their plushy stables,

that I was too cocky, too out of line,
too unbecoming for an indentured
scullion or too unconvinced
that everything this nimbused country does
to other star-crossed nations is only
God's mandate?

Was it really fair to my three sisters to battle
with my mother's unruly blood pressure
& for them to be running frantically
to catch a taxi to take her to emergency room
when my mother let go
a rivulet of nose bleed
& her sari turned soaking wet with wild rubies

while I feuded with a blonde country
saying after every bloody face off & gig

thank God I am still gasping,
thank God I can still taste

my fresh blood
from lacerated lips,

Thank God I am still standing
on my two undaunted feet

& can still hear the knotted thump
of my beleaguered heart
& twenty years cantered past

as an ill-begotten, un-bravoed aria.

POET IN LAHORE'S ANARKALI BAZAAR

If I were a Botticelli,
I would have painted you
as a gilded Venus rising
from a tropical lotus
& let the whole world bite its lips,
singe its groins staring
at your primrose flesh.

If I were the Emperor Shah Jehan,
I would have impregnated you
at least a dozen times to clone
stunning images of your
unblemished palm beach beauty.

I would have built a Taj Mahal
to frame your red begonia grace
but I am just a down on my luck
petit bourgeois bard short on patience
& breath & Pak rupees & hazing with sweat

& haggling ad nauseam to chip off
the starting price of this meta-gorgeous
lilac sari polka dotted with silver stars,
crescents & mythic animals

while feuding with the seedy whiff
of a rotten melon crossed with the fresh droppings
of an addled, adrift, aging, scimitar-horned cow
in this sweltering bazaar perched on a sizzling noon

embellished by the bracing doggerels, wheedling prayers
& spitfire wailing of the hearty beggars, whistling bicycles,
grunting trucks counterpointed by sassy busses,
swaggering motorcycles, meandering taxis, sidling
donkey carts, gaudily-painted motor-rickshaws
& their drivers wearing sweat-glossed *shalwar-kameez*
hustling like little whores in Diamond Bazaar
for euro, yen & dollar rich tourists.

Requiem For A Muse

Her self-possession,
like Persian buttercup blossoms,
will now embellish the heavens.

Our snagged hearts are heavy with
melancholy's straitjackets.

The moon flickers as a nervous lark hanging
over the bulbs of laurel fig trees.

The Jacaranda tree of night hasn't calmed
the nerves of the fidgeting streets.

The smudgy sign of Al-Medina Kebab Hotel
blinks & flutters like a rapidly racing heart.

The vibrato of our voices is dimmed
by a jingling clock of snipes.

We take her jasmine-draped body
in our carmine Toyota truck

to be smothered by cinnamon gravel
& dirt & a bushel of rose petals.

She is already enshrined in our heads
like Schumann's *Piano Quintet in E flat.*

The mailman found her slouched body
under death's boulder, saw a frantic truck

leaving like a robber
in a shroud of blue delphiniums.

Her electric demitasse auguring eyes are loosened
like gems & tire-marked, the taffeta thighs

on which I had my love prayers so often
are cracked like pelted glass.

Begonia navel purpled & slashed, the verbena-red
Garbo lips no keener now than the laden breeze.

The oleander hands that tuned my sex for best bowing
are now hyacinth-blue & laced with mud-sashes.

Stilled is the quiet fire of those blue acanthus eyes.

Torn is her azalea left shoulder, blasted is her
vignettes' diorama, her sweet wisecracking intellect.

Halted are desire's dilating floods & flash points
that fire up my loins over six years.

Her silken shawl is a funnel cloud
of crushed flaming trumpets,

Her moth-orchid mouth is a tainted jewel,

her whiter than meadowsweet body
already melting in death's sulfuric acid.

God Almighty, where is your amazing grace?

Where is your magic baton
to turn humble anthills into swallowtails?

Lord God please stare hard
at the done in heaven of my muse.

I can't help but curse
your terrible camera tricks.

Harvest Of Gods

Milling about Rome's piazzas & moped-inured streets,
watching uniformed gendarmes flirting
with every cute unescorted belle,
you also take in flotillas of fountains,
the Rococo heavens of marble & gaiety,
the Baroque raptures hewn in stone & myth-lore
& you are easily tempted to exude—

"Yes, there is a God & that God is Bernini,"
& a week later in Amsterdam you are scorched
by Rembrandt's sardonic glare who wants you
to acknowledge his regal credentials
& you gladly oblige in equally hyperbolic raves.

In a visit to Brussels Rubens titillates you
by the Brigitte Bardot gleam of his wife's skin
& you are ready to eat your words & concede
"There are Gods other than Bernini who are equally splendid."

Jordeans, Poussin, Vermeer & Velasquez
hold you in a corner
like the hard selling carpet peddlers of Istanbul
to display their gilded wares, their gaggle of wonders.
You are left speechless by Caravaggio's
fugues of light & savage beauty
& then again you recognize how reckless you were
in your giddy pedestrian applause
when the fountains of Rome had first
whispered to your so tenderly.

The endless candelabra of nature hums & flares
with a thousand quasars & galaxies.
In an hour's spasms & turns,
a dozen suns are hatched & weaned,
some infant galaxies quickly dispatched
to screaming nurseries. Byron, Darwin or Frans Hals
are minor evangelists & little hawkers
of a brazen & wastrel nature—ever churning, ever gravid,
with swelling nipples & tingling ovaries
never sated or cool with the latest litter of gods.

At The Airport Lounge

I am sitting in the Shangrila hotel lounge, waiting.
My daughter is flying in from Barcelona
& who do I see walking in the lounge
in a delirium-draped haze
of a frosty November afternoon?

It is you, Maggie Bloom;
you have become a little plump
& pudgy-cheeked but nothing else
about your bio emporium is off kilter.
You don't recognize me wearing
my baldness, dark glasses

& graying beard with a sly frown.
My eyes caress your statuesque frame
& then turn back to my ring-less hand
wrapped around a highball of whisky.
I must look like a rueful, exiled God
a little besotted, gazing at his lost Shangrila.

In a drizzle of dredged up reminiscences
my heart reels watching you lift
that gold-rimmed cup of tea
to your star-fruit lips.
That auburn smile is still tangy fresh
like mulled red wine tinged with
cloves & cinnamon.
I still remember how you could recite my damasked
but flawed & not yet annealed poems
better than me considering
my swarthy accent—

you, a scented full-figured dream
with red cascade of curls,
recalling other less perfect
dreams such as my poems.

In those alchemical moments of recitals
the pretty medium would become
the very subterfuge of poetry

as if a swinging ballerina had become
the life-dance of Vishnu
& all the half-charred memories
of candle-light embraces,
henna-dipped traces on the walls
of my fifty-five-dollar loft
at Madison Campus

are now pouring down to become
a gagging knot in my middle-aged throat
as if I am stargazing
through the Kitt Peak telescope,
the far off nebulas & galaxies.

Do you remember any of that?
It has been twenty-six years to be exact
but why should you bother with scuttling ghosts?

Your visage looks so Saturn-happy
but I can still recall one hyacinth afternoon
when your eyes brimmed with pearls
at my wily hinting that my Shiite mother
doesn't like white women
& worst of all the Jewish ones

& how you had torn up my mother's picture
in a blush of frenzy
as if you were slashing the wrists of a bad omen
& I had slapped your face hard enough
that you had sobbed for an hour.

How should I begin or end—
how can limping words lift
this galleon of pain,
how should I phrase
without a shadow of sour grapes:

Your savage beauty
still the tangerine bloom of calla lilies

purling over the soft pastels
of this hotel lounge,

your eyes still the searing Olga
with sepia hungers,
the ruby tips still the rim cones
of your fingers
& your pianissimo giggling
still the flaming georgette
dyed in saffron & pomegranate,
the blue bird scarf still burns
in the rose-glow of your violet cleavage,

your caution still the sagacious calm
of a savanna lioness.

Those three teenage girls
fawning over you, I presume
are your spoiled daughters.

Let me be blunt, they are not as radiant as you
& you can slap me hard for saying that.

Are they the young countesses practicing
your dowager empress charms,
watching over your forbidden kingdom?

They are all dressed up
in my endearing monarda scarlet.

Is that just a coincidence
or part of a cosmic stratagem!

Good riddance, they never learnt my scent
& your sweet face has no nail marks
of my presence or absence

Aren't you glad that I let you leave
in my dumb star-lust
& you never slipped back
to my Medusa's alcove?

TWO BROTHERS AT PLAY

Nana, in your recent snaps I see you wearing
a checkered lungi & undershirt,
& propped by colored bolsters
you have become a blanched
filigree of bones & your face
a gaudy fretwork of wrinkles,
your skinny feet—
a wire mesh of tulip tubers,
& Daphne-white is the raging tint
of your mane & awning brows,
& the stiffness of your carriage presages
the gripping vise of rigor mortis
that wows & spooks us all.

My dear old scraggy aunt kids on the phone
about the pell-mell of your pills:
a peacock blue to jumpstart the sluggish enzymes,
a lily-mauve to jangle the deep torpor,
an allium-gold to derail emphysema's rams,
a gardenia-white to quell the stormy heartbeats
a sunflowery one to pinion depression's fairy—
all the glaring signposts that a wheezing universe
is not yet ready to bail out or throw in the towel!

Nana, it was in your baroque library
that flirted with a Napoleon's bust like a heresy,
& lined with leather-bound books in gold,
copra & columbine tints & harbored
a framed smile of a toothless Gandhi,
the dangling fetus of a tiger cub
in an airtight mason jar on a mahogany stand
& against the pastel yellow high walls,
ebony & ivory colored floor,
expansive French windows,
drone of crickets, shrieks of koels,
waft of jasmine, mulberry, eucalyptus,
lemon trees, sprawling mints swooping
through the paisley curtains
& under the dusty Persian chandeliers,
mounted heads of cheetahs, Bengal tigers,

Himalayan stags with cellophane stares
that I first met the gilded ghosts
of Bertrand Russell & D. H. Lawrence
in frail mirrors of tired dusty books.
While I was there, for my birthday you got me
Tagore's *Gitanjali* & I fancied that the poet
was a quivering bride waiting
in her crimson gold sari,
for her heavenly groom, by her
rose-petal-draped sandalwood bed
& I devoured that thistle of a volume
like a teen-age girl hooked
on star-gooseberry chutney.

On my final day at your mansion I swiped
from your library Malraux's *Man's Hope*
to fatten my low-life bookshelf in Karachi.
I was then just a sapling so untutored
in the mores, mirages, mysteries
& witchcrafts of language.
That was the last time
I ever shook your hands,
polka-danced along your
cypress-vine blossomed soul
& floated my teen-age monologues
on the pontoon bridge of your
half-approving, half-sardonic smirk.

After that summer's long splash
my family went back
to Sind's cactus-flared landscape
dotted with neem, pipal, jamun trees,
chestnut-colored hills,
galling heat & bubbling shores
licked pearl-white by the Arabian Sea.
After that time in Bihar Province
our shadows never crossed.

I left home to find my perch
in a world that was never still.
I became an errant Apollo
in a suntanned vagabondage.

There were sweaty rickshaws,
jammed ferries, crowded subway trains,
mammoth planes to be caught in time & missed,
there were meds for typhoid, malaria & hypertension
to be filled & dropped
& girls with currant-jam tongues
to be picked & won & lost & wept over.
There were bloody rendezvous with part-time thugs,
muggers, vicious skinheads
as the tests of endurance & manhood.
There was nervous pacing for the auditions,
interviews, rejection slips

& there was the patient honing of treachery
& sweet cunning & its hundred facelifts
that becomes our civilized coat of arms
& the manic overdrive to tease out
the eels of a fleeting fame.
Nana, you too once flashed a mustache of ambition.
You were the Nabob of Khagra—the honorable member
of Bihar's parliament but you never became
the "honorable chief minister"
& I never became the hot shot mandarin
being mobbed & plagued by *L'Monde*'s
or *The New York Time*'s paparazzi.

Remember, you repackaged
Swift's quote for me once—
"When a true man of genius graces this world,
all the dunces get busy to conspire against his arse."
Consider all the dumplings & dimsums of slights
& catcalls we had ignored in our hunted youths for being
so weird & difficult & then think how we had sought
comfort in Swift's soothing aphorism.

But over time we too became under-driven,
too bloated with our own incantations.
In my jarring twenties I became a rag tag
troubadour, a small time Ghazal jockey
& was considered someone with elm-high promise

& then I had to leave the country
under the fundamentalist threats.

In the new country I lost myself completely
in immigrant shuffle
& started my penance like Sisyphus
for the sins of mating
& now every cattleya calyx of dreams
that I had pined for flaps on reverie's walls
like a maudlin seascape in a cheap Wal-Mart frame.

Nana, I am now a middle-aged man
& you have just turned eighty-three & all the reckless
bluster & peacock buffoonery of our youth
that confounded our rivals, charmed our friends
& mortified our parents has abandoned us
as the old paint leaves a time-lapped Ford truck,
as a kept mistress quits on her bankrupt lover,
& all the stolen & bartered coronets & tiaras
of wisdom can't save us
from the mounting dunes of hours.

Nana, in our nagging bones,
in our ticking temples,
the shrill tomorrows howl
like the squealing sirens of police cars,
blaring steamers, long-winded cargo trains.
My memory is going slowly blind
in amnesia's sandstorm

& I hear that mussels of Alzheimer's
are now your daily repast.

We are now what we are—
landlocked & moat-broken
& our fickle becoming is eager to fold
& crash in being's boggy everglades.

The bitter seeds of finality sizzle
on our palates & we relish every sashayed glance

of a lovely face with such catatonic abandon
as if the core of the world is going to melt
in the dribbles of our sentences
& all the scarlet gerbera daisies,
stunning Birds of Paradise,
purple chemisettes of Jacaranda blossoms
can no longer calm our erratic hearts
that once used to overtake us.

Nana, it tickles me to death to feel
in my fitful reflexes,
in the sibilance of my consonants

that now we both are ocean bound
& air marked to capsize & drown,
that either one of us could go first

& the bumbling business of biding time
may go suddenly bust.

Our distant promenades
have finally intersected,
the difference in our ages,

sights & hearings no longer figure
in this harrowing calculus.

Nana, under the canopy of a leering Kali
we both are now helpless as Rio's forsaken kids

trekking the killing streets in dirty underwear,

we both are now finally brothers, mighty pale

& ramshackled & yet playing hard

the macabre game,

the waiting game,

the baiting game!

MY USELESS PASSION

Oh language! the arpeggio dance
of my red-ginger blood,
it is only you that I have lusted & wooed
in all my courtships of rivers, flaming
glorybowers & suave women,
it was you that I have hungered for
in my nocturnal plunderings
of the tombs of old Titans of arts,
in all my sweet basal, savory,
rosemary indulgences.
I have only sought & yearned
your nectarine nape & your thyme blossom arms.

All the ravishing girls that caused me giddiness
were just the sweet decoys, cunning proxies
for your insufferable beauty, for your primrose
tiramisu tongue. Only the good runes & cantos
in your kohl-rimmed pearl-green eyes
have emblazoned my blood.
The measures of my heart were always synced
to the rise & fall of your strawberry sun,
your hundred & one pseudonyms & charms
that I have invented to serenade the "wow" women
were just the shrewd ruses to steal kisses & caresses
from your runaway splendor.

It is to your toned gait & tanned gaiety
to which I have always surrendered
& come back to your Ashanti clicks & Kabuki masks.
It is towards you that I have scuffed & lurched
in all the igniting dawns & gazpacho red sunsets,
in my ravings & silences I have echoed nothing
but your madness & screaming quietude,
you—the glorious temple whore—
the gorgeous Mae West, the licentious Collette;
you have been my impossible passion
since I was six & heard your glissando moanings
in the ghazals of the best Urdu poets
reciting their painted raptures
on the Lucknow public radio!

A Painter's Dilemma

How many times I have calmed myself by musing
that when I leave your allegro side, your bed
dappled with candytuft blossoms & white irises,
there would be no scarlet penstemon
clouds of longings.

That you will find other friendly men
& paramours to forge long lasting bonds
& unions & I will wash off my anguish
by other vermilion lips, toadflax bulbs of bras
& we will become once again
fading sub-texts of some crazy dream for each other.

But then how do I know for sure
this will exactly happen as scripted,
that nothing would go wrong or awry
between the rose-hearted coreopses of my hopes
& the black mondo grasses of my despair
that the universe will stay on an even keel.

But how do I know when once I have banished you
from my frolicking frescos & murals,
I would be able to lure you back
to inhabit them again?

You are no God or sun-fleece
or shower of tasseled stars
or diamond-dusted waterfalls
that keep blessing me as long as
I agree to breathe & watch.

What if you cordially decline
to lounge again in my languorous
paintings like an odalisque
even if I threaten to kill myself?

In Praise Of Solipsism

When I crooned about
the faint fugues of the stars
& their ruptured veins flickering
like the emblazoned neon lips
hanging by a nightclub entrance
in downtown Amsterdam,

when I sang of the merry-go-round
of the heart racing galaxies
pegged to light year metronome,

when I cawed about
the fabulous correspondence
between the birds of paradise
& the painted bride of Saturn,

when I groaned about
the lancet of a twister
entrancing a Texan township,

when I embellished
my lyrics with the terrific
swagger of a black mamba
ready to lasso her poisonous jets,

when I keened my dirge
for the Tootsi cadavers
washing ashore
under the Rwandan sun
& the clouds of swarming flies
and famished birds,

when I sang of the tar blotches
on God's Melanomic cheeks & forehead
& his broken heart by the mewlings
of the scared stiff
& starving Kossavars
in a picture perfect Diaspora
on their way to furrow-browed,
dun mountains or death,

when I caroled about the neighborhood imps
& trick-or-treating rascals
in bloodcurdling outfits ringing my doorbell
& besting an inquisition matinee,

when I sang beloved lavishly
of your sorceress eyes,
that could stun a crowd
delirious by Italian wines
gallantly singing a Puccini aria
along a racy accordion
by Rome's Trevi fountains,

when I crooned about your arched
red lips dipped
as if in peach schnapps & burgundy mums
& your silver thighs gyring me
closer & deeper
to the tufted eye of your rapture,

when I bragged of Archangel
as if he was my Shabbat boy
ironing my dark purple shirt
& faded black jeans & watering
my crimson spider lilies
& snap dragons
& polishing my scuffed wing-tips

believe me, beloved,

I was singing of no others

but only of myself!

BLESSED EMPTINESS

Rachael, you may vividly remember
when I come home & straggle through
the webbed expanse of the house—

the stucco patio, the blessed square
of the backyard garden,
the lavender-green bedroom,
the long sprawling hallway,
the sun-dappled kitchenette,

the laid back pantry, the laundry alcove
tight like a locked jaw,

but I can't find your aunt's scent
or the talisman of her glinty voice
I feel this sudden gash of unease,

this sharp scythe of wariness,
hanging like a panicked moon,
& a pulse of emptiness starts ticking
till she is once again ensconced
in my circumference

& I feel I am back in my element,
that I am sitting snugged tight
in my sanguine universe.
You may call it love,
addiction or obsession
in the rude lexicon of shrinks

but if your boyfriend can't feel
even this blessed stab of emptiness
when you are away from his gaze
then what good is his coinage of love
in clichéd & clinched words?
What good is your ring-less hand
tired of waiting?

What good are your cyclamen dreams
of rapture in his reluctant arms?

Strange Tidings

Isn't it scandalous & spooky,
my accidental friend
whom I have just met at Borders,

that all the six important Eves in my life:
my mother, my wife,
my daughter, my three sisters
wouldn't lose a tiny salamander of sleep

if all the prodigious cache
of my verses might turned brackish
like bones in a crematorium.

They wouldn't permit themselves
an hour of mourning for my life's work

so I wonder by what freakish twist of nature

I was bequeathed to such vapid strangers.

Isn't it another glaring proof of the rumor

that God is not a good matchmaker
that marriages are really made in hell

that Camus is born to a mute mother,
that Toulouse-Lautrec is squeezed shut
by achondroplasia

& Byron remains clubfooted
even in his glowing obituaries,

that I am stuck with a sieve-memory
I culled from my Mommy Dearest.

Hence we raise our hoarse voices to grouse
about God's obscene mismatches!

BREVITY

I may suffer from knotted gasps,
& my ears may ring
with the presto buzz of hypertension

but there is no shortness of squall
in my poetry's ravishing sails.

I sing ballads of whales,
canticles of erotic mermaids who breakfast
& tango as trumpeter swans
on sun-jeweled mornings.

I can recall perfectly the songs
of Columbus' shipmates
glaring at the colonnades of somnambulant
corn-flowered Atlantic waves.

I croon about a haggard
& bronzed Odysseus
with strawberry blond hair
going back to a noise-riddled home
smelling of Penelope's suitors' sweat,
schooners of wines & walloping bladders,

so don't tell me shortness is splendid
& brevity has star power.

I am the siren of history's
ruched incantations.

I am the walking liturgy of Mother Earth.

I am the painter of boy-Alexander's cherry-red dreams;

I will use as much opulence of silk taffeta
words as I need to sash a river's pomp
& bluster, to saddle a young rapid's mare
or reign in a pubescent typhoon!

INVITE BACK

In the damp, half-shaded breeze
great cowslips doze over the flaming mimulus,
the orange brigade of leopard lilies flaunt
their tiaras in a crash of monarchs.

Insurgent angel trumpets float above
the slumping lavender rains.

Red hot tulips dance a cool swing
in a lake of impatiens & refrain.

A band of humming birds crashes in
to court the bee balm groupies.

The lumbering moon still fancies
the tufted phlox, the ocher dianthus
waves like babes in strollers.

Meadow sage still glows in a silk tulle reverie.

So nothing has changed in my little world
of repeatable dreams since you walked out
of that enclosed front porch
in an Orson Wells-size tantrum.

I still have that half empty bottle
of Chablis in the frig
so e-mail or call some time to reassure me
that you have already forgotten
the petty toadflax squabble
that had us stomping our feet
by those gold-streaked yarrows,
red-blue grass peas
& pistachio-green leaves early last week.

"Every thing is so flippant against such
heartbreaking awning of splendor!"

I tell you these are your own words, mister!

A SONATINA

It is summer. We are strolling on the beach
as if a funeral is pulling our strings.

We are oblivious to the nip & snap of stiletto wind.
A snow-rose, transvestite moon
shows stress of endless stalking
& moves like a hearse carriage.

A whiny petulant wind throws a mild tantrum.
Even though I am holding your hand
I feel as if I am grabbing a ghost's wrist.

An off duty beach-guard in faded corduroy jeans
& dark glasses is courting a trumpet—
music is losing its head in its bejeweled pageantry.

On the beach by the low enclosing wall
couples grow bolder in the paisley darkness—
knees pine for knees, hands lunge for breasts,
lovelier & firmer than any tulip glasses.

Swimmers are cresting on corrugating waves.
Air is turning pimento-red by lovers' soldering kisses,
lust builds sweltering nests in steamy vines

but screaming tears are tearing our eyes
& our veiled voices are playing
proxies for our plummeted faces.

I have just told you that this love of yours
is too sapping, too enervating,
too expensive for me to bear
& we have decided to become strangers
to each other.

While the bleached concourse of waves
mock our penitent silence,

we part company as two convicts
who haven't prayed for ages.

YOU AND HE

I don't know exactly how you really feel
when I whisk & float through
your wet grape-hyacinth heavens
as a drunken falcon
or how you gasp when I raise
the temps of your teats
till they become pent up blossoms
& the tides in your humid honeycombs
are plashed in a flame vine rapture.

I can only guess the arc of pleasure
searing in your wide-shut eyes like an electric surge,

I can only glance its glimmer
in your implacable limbs rustling
in a comatose-drift,

in your velvet back turning into
dogwood blossoms,
in the caress of your bee balm tongue
combing my palette,
then how, beloved, could God possibly guess
what I go through on a daily basis unless

he grazes on my ruminant grounds,
peers in my abyss of rage & dread,
aches through my jaded snagged heart,
suffers the pull & tear
of my immigrant flesh,

wallows in the shame pits of my sloth
& dares to ride the A-train
of my hooded KKK nightmares

Don't you surmise beloved:
This is quite an impossible trip for a prudish,
Semitic God who can't even spell *Kama Sutra*!

A VISION

She comes to lie with me
flaunting her enigmatic Mona Lisa smile
in an African robe of electric
tangerine terrycloth
over a purple Donatella Versace bra,
in a sequined blue Cashmere sweater,
in a faded lilac Pashmina scarf,
in red satin organza thong panties.

Her curled puff-scone lips brushed
with the lipstick of Mauiian dawns,
her small chin is soft as sparrow's tongue,
her voice mellifluous as Regina Carter's
riffing violin, her dimples are flushed with Irish lilies,
her nails glazed with the blood of poppies,
her eyes glinting with liquid radium,
her gold loop earrings kindling the sage
green air, her jeweled nose with a diamond ring
prettier than Halle Berry's.

her long legs a feast of flamingo candy,
her ankles tinkling with silver bracelets,
her tresses shimmer like cobra's rings.
She is wearing her purple gold babouches
& I unrobe her swank moons with my
fretful fingers & tug on her magnolia breasts
till they are sore & big like palm blossoms
& I pluck on the rose cellos of her rump,
& we make love as famished leopards & our moans
& giggles tease the sensors of the fire alarms

& the queen bed shimmies & hollers
as if rocked by Saddam's tantrums
& then a neon-blue lassitude
drizzles as opium & mists my clanging senses
& I close my eyes
to receive the last caress of my vagrant mistress,
& drink the long French kiss
of my beloved, my long awaited death.

POETRY READING AT BORDERS'S BOOKSTORE

Our rapt listeners:
You patient eavesdroppers, cunning voyeurs,
slick surfers of our lathyrus-blue waves
who get foggy-eyed & high
listening to our delirious lines,
you avaricious alley cats who sniff our
delusions' treated meats,
you savor the succulent pastries
of our over-painted raptures,
our over-rouged melancholies.
You tune in for our stardust fanfares
doctored often to give them a regal jaw,
a Nordic nose bridge,
the jewels of Keira Knightley's eyes,
a Naomi Campbell navel

& cheeks blushed up
to shame gerber daisies.
You come here to see the mug shots
of our twisted souls wallowing
in technicolor epilepsy
over the brimming demitasses of Espresso,
Cappuccino & coffee crested
with Dutch chocolate
against the clanging boorishness
of cash registers
& you balance each shimmering dime
of our inebriated staves
on the waxen brows or breast scales
of your personal ironies

& decide like an accountant
which dime to drop
which quarter to slip
in your memory's deep pockets.
You cheap shot gamblers, junkies
of our tainted elegance,
trying to hit the jackpot
for the price of a coffee cup

& hustling to learn in a crash course
how not to bet your whole life savings
on a stillborn dream,
how not to host the wolf of impotence
by daily embrace of straight whiskies,
how not to blow entire evenings
grooming, fumbling, fretting
mumbling which fleece top,
which denim jeans, which voile scarf,
which pair of gold-rimmed shoes
best match the maroon leather jacket,
which French perfume will outlast the red cactus
tequila raptures & the cherry martinis,
which after-shave will disarm
the wary date taking her finals in two days,
which eyeliner will reign in
the shrew evening,
which lipstick will hold him hostage
till dawn flashes its camellia grin
& yet knowing quite plainly
there is no pearl earring message
tagged to the answering machine,
no lover half-dead or living
who has written or spoken
in 8 months, there is no hot knock
to singe the chilled entrance,
no gorge of a rendezvous
to stick your tongue in,
no shoulder of a sage or a saint
to cry on & stanch your anguish!

BRIDGE ON GRAND RIVER

Bridges are languid sphinxes
that undulate on the supernal waves of memories.
They manage to outlive & out-trance
the pubescence of our widgeon hopes,
the waltzes of our frets & fears,
the diasporic curlews of our dreams,
the ripped strands
of our lovers' camisoles
still holding the faint scents
of forgotten dates.

Bridges remain impervious
to squalls' squealing scripts,
the smoked greasy dialects of buses,
scudding cars, scampering semi-trucks.

They out-grin our cacophonous
obituaries that jealously guard
our miseries, failures & fault lines.

Bridges melt in fogs like salts,
finally lost & washed off
like ghosts & goblins
in our memory's crowded throngs.
I don't know if this bridge
on Grand River,
now stone deaf to the overtures
of stampeding police cars
& school buses,
had already taken over his humble office
before the blasted JFK's
pomegranate-brain
on a Dallas boulevard
& its pods were all over
Jackie's fuchsia dress

or if this bridge had cut its teeth
before Martin Luther King Junior
knelt down in a pool
of lavender martyrdom.

This bridge has grown old,
tired & stubbled with grime & psoriasis
while hobnobbing with prickly sun
& the hobo moon
& lusting after wanton rains.
Its perforated gables are
fading bookmarks,
its rusted beams, fatigued curvatures,
fraying cement scars show its age,
its morphed skeleton is like the carcass
of an ancient croc,
its pachydermic gums showing markings
of nervous grunts, brutal dental work,
& constant howling of hysterical years.
Its shoulders hint at wind's perennial raids,
hundred scabs like scuzzy irises
have grown all over
its dappled scalp but he can't see
that he is an Oedipus sobbing
for the milk of forgiveness.

Every day I cruise down to work
by this old hunchbacked behemoth
against the looming clothesline of maples,

I wonder when my own tiptoed
withering will speed up
& dash to overtake
the invisible passing
of this unassuming, congenial bridge.

EXUBERANCE

He always saw his father's fury
dancing like an avalanche
ever testing his quivering
primrose jasmine nerves
& he figured one day he too would
grow up to be a force of nature—

violent, effervescent,
most lethal & spectacular—
like a bullet train
braided with electric storms

& all the tulips, gardenias & irises
would be in absolute awe of him.

So you, Jim Jericho, with your thick trifocals,
wiry hair, heavy jowl, wispy moustache,
saturnine mouth, Ganesha nose & gunny bag
of stale gossips & you overly churlish Sarah Serengeti
in your mid-fifties with sagging tits,
upturned brows & pursed lips
who is losing scalp hair faster
than your balding husband
are those scared, quivering garden flowers

& I can't do much to calm your jostled nerves.

Just pray that my soul is soon yanked out
by a silver-rimmed angel as I prayed tearfully
to Allah to call back my daddy
when I was only six years old

& was routinely humbled & bedeviled
by his chugging cockscomb rage

or you may try to get used to my exuberance
& it's attendant mayhems as one gets used to

tyrant typhoons & implacable flashfloods.

MY BROTHER'S NOSE

We were the true salt & pepper of the earth;
in other words we were pantry poor.
My brother had an eerie gift of smell.
We fondly called him a mesmerizing kitchen rat.
He had, we siblings surmised,
just a couple less odor receptor proteins
than the house mice in gray jeans.
The olfactory bulb in his brain,
we quipped, was bigger than the church bell.
We all banked on his amazing talent
for spying goodies & delicacies mother will
squirrel away for the honored guests.

My brother grew up to be a chemist
but not for too long, he did quit after he caught
the giddying whiff of Lenin & Mao
& revolutions bloody & bloodless
became his nose-candies
& I became a poet in elusive search of scents
of doe-eyed beauties wearing fragrances
of mignonettes, alyssums & blue lilacs.

I WISH I COULD BOAST

I wish I could boast like Marie Curie
without batting my eyes that my art
is my fondest caviar & my hottest sex tonic
& aphrodisiac but I can't mouth such blatant fibs.
They don't suit my temperament & gene map.

Yes, I will step out without fanfare or alibi
from the eye of a stormy poem
to savor the slow-dance of my palate
against the heavenly cardamom-tinged
Baklava pastry flaked & glistening
as a Marc Jacob's blonde model
& yes I will wrestle you, beloved,
till you lay bare on my king size bed
to delight in a brunette Reese Witherspoon rapture.
The poem must wait her turn in the blushing queue.

A HYPHENATED LIFE

He lives in a hyphenated cocoon
buoyed by orange, dark plum,
neon-purple plumes of smells from fried
aubergine, okra, spiced lintels sautéed with
garlic, cumin seeds, curry powder,
a wash of turmeric, coriander & ginger.
He is losing with every marooned breath
another shaft, another barb, another quill
of his old cultural feathering—
letting go the faux yodeling, yelps, snarls
of his juvenile Bollywood villains
& matinee bullies splashing
from the honey-custard movie screens
of his fond Lucknow & Barayli.
His memory is slowly losing its octopus grip
over the euphonious antics of the dashing heroes
& heartthrob starlets of his seaside Karachi teens.
Now in the States he smuggles his blue-poppy fancy
through the warp & distillate of a hijacked language.

He wrings robustly its wet chemisette
till the weak-kneed, slack-limbed, menopausal
parts of speech start dripping with fresh blood
in a leap of faith. His daily grunting gigs
as a bard apprentice in English are heartbreaking.
He hurls his deckled words like a marine drill sergeant
as if hoping some day their power will break
tyrants, raise shimmering portals
more lasting than hills, more final than fate,
while dealing with cortisol spiking stress
of earning a living in IT's bytes-swishing lanes,
getting the warped car engine head fixed
& then making the frantic dash to supermarket
to buy fat free milk & then cooking in the evening
the favored Thai dish for his teen-age son
& yet he is ever tingling with obscene itch
to smooch the night phlox nape of a blond
language that his ancestors never used
to rage or sue or curse or make love or pray
or banter or bash or blaspheme!

THEY JUST COME

Slender jet-fountains—sob their ecstasies.
                    —Paul Verlaine

In my poems, dear reader, you will find
the gold-tinseled dust-sashes
of jaded caravanserais
of old Shiraz & Esfahan,
sassy solipsisms & big-breasted come-ons
of Marilyn Monroe & Madonna,
the choking sadness
of Billie Holiday & Sade,
the mango-sweetness
of Rimbaud & Marvin Gaye,

the stunning disguise of a speckled
emperor moth with a painted hind wing
with a mammalian face
& shimmering pupils to ward off his foes.

Actually I can't tell you
what you might run into
tiptoeing their fox-glove dreams
& cloying nightmares.

My poems never ask for my blessing
for their hundred saxifrage charades
& curlicued camouflages.

They just come like painted rock-stars
high on hubris & Angel Dust.

A Poem For Mr. Charles Darwin

Mr. Darwin: It is not where we are coming from
but where we are heading to
that counts.
It is because Mr. Newton is wading the piano keys,
Mr. Shakespeare is caressing the tenor sax,
Mr. Proust is gracing the bass
& Mr. Picasso is flaming the silver trumpet
that our glittering quartet looks better
than Jupiter & Mars.

That one day we may all be inhumed in ground
but we are not just some cairns of bones.
Our extinction will only herald
that we just grew tired of our greatness
& took a long sabbatical.

It is our mad dog curiosity,
the long guns of our puissance,
& our scarlet-sage exuberance
that make our psalms sweeter
than the songs of cactus finches,
our speeches more sturdy
than the armored iguanas,
our deliveries more robust
than the giant tortoises you rode
bare backed in the Galapagos island.

It is our forward march that gets us such high marks
that Apollo & Zeus come to our poetry readings.
That gods quote verbatim from our chapbooks.
Even though our mortality is terminal,
our fancy pries open the universe's thick petals.
Let me tell you a fey secret.
We were the ones who really commanded—
Let there be light
& all the galaxies complied!

THE PRODIGIOUS RAIN

Perhaps it will help you
if I confess at the outset
that I am a writer first & then a poet.
As sure as I am of the drumming tides
in my anarchist blood,
I think the measure of a writer's greatness
is never the length or dwarfishness
of his works like a lover's electric spathe.
I adore both Proust & Rilke
who sit close to each other
on the exuberance pyramid
but Proust is a greater shaman
than Rilke since Proust never controlled
the tango of his exuberance
& made for himself & for us
a more shimmering prodigious rain
that so lushly soaks each petal, each anther
of his bougainvillea novels
& the pearl-flecked cheeks of our thanks.

ROBERT FROST

You sought your safe haven
in the pensive schools of peregrinas
& mountain ashes, in holly-fern's
flowing hands, in the gilded cotton bales
gleaming as Jane Mansfield's golden steins.
You found your Shangrila in the bearded willows
& rococo yellows of cottonwoods,
in the red scrub-oaks, in the assorted orchids
of neuroses & madness of pastoral folks
while I plod & map-quest through my urban purgatory
loathing with blitheless heart your flashy, luxuriant,
anodyne & mallow eclogues
& though I can easily recall like a spelling bee
all my showy urban plusses over you,
I have this disquieting feeling
that *I* am the overworked famished farmhand
languishing by your kitchen door
& you are the cheerful, chatty,
charitable-matron pitying my lousy luck.

THE PASSAGE

Beloved: I have known you for six long months
yet I didn't know that you are
close friend with bronchitis,
that you once had such a huge crush on Elvis Presley,
that you had a thimble shaped scar on your left butt.
& you still get nightmares about your uncle Ted
who hanged himself when you were just twelve.
There is so little that I know about you & your dreams

& there is so little other galaxies know about us
& with no scold, frown, sigh or a complimentary grin,
time passes us by as if
nothing of this has ever mattered.

THE SEASHELLS

When we are gone, beloved,
all that will remain are these
whispering seashell poems—
these sweet clover serenades
of our longings,
our flowering tobacco red feuds,
our lilac makeups,
our limonia arrivals & dreaded
light-year departures,
the green pipewort gleams of your eyes
quivering like candle heads
& my hands gunning for your orchid breasts
& a little girl's anxious dulcet voice
on the bedroom door begging
like spring breeze:

Please, please, may I come in
I have something to show you,
it will just take two seconds?

Mary's Lobelia Blues

My neighbors fret out loud—why I sometimes cruise my red Seville in circles around the sub-division like a dancing dervish. I thought all departures were also arrivals or because I don't keep my calendar in my car—my lodestone, my Delphic oracle that insinuates what the next day will bring or take or trade.

The neighbors think that I am a doddering fool because I knock off the same stony homily over & over as an idiot-savant or a cockatoo. May be, I love my cadence like some bards unwilling to surrender an open mike.
I admit at times I mis-stack days. I make Friday stalk Wednesday without the footbridge of a Saturday so I don't follow the tedium of inter-laced days too closely. Does that make me a downright heretic or an apostate?
My neighbors claim I sometimes appear by their doorsteps not knowing what I am after & then I follow them to their trucks & cars. Why are they so jealous of their solitude? The other day I couldn't recall my own name but why should I tell them *my* name when they know it is emblazoned on my mailbox like the Pleiades webbed in the stars.

They accuse me of stealing from their mailboxes. That I embellish my mantelpiece with their valentine cards. They say my lies keep multiplying like the excessive egg-laying of cockatiels. Don't I have the civil right to spout harmless lies like a minister who spins his fictions about God's son & his fabulous nepotism? I don't think there is anything amiss with me. I eat, I sleep, I cheat lavishly whenever I can, playing gin rummy, poker, table-tennis or solitaire.

My neighbors call this handsome young man in blue parka & pixie haircut my only son. He is supposed to move me to his home to spare me from the social services *worrycrats*, but what if he butchers me like a bison & stores my body parts in his frig & start eating them chop by chop? I hear others often whisper *dementia*. I don't know its meaning but I wonder if it is some kind of charming butterfly, a black & white swallowtail dappled with blue pearls, & if so one must never shear its wings & let the rabid winds hoist & steer it towards the daisy-white hills & when it gets there let it vanish quill by quill by the salvia rapture of thirst & hypothermia. If I were a butterfly I would prefer that exit route, that swell ending.

CHANGE OF FORTUNE

I was a fire breather once.
Made fun of falling decals & cowries of stars
as if they were failed jokers.
I would laugh my heart out at the sallow moon
for his pale lantern.

My whooshing blazes were famous & spectacular
like pansy orchids and Waikiki beach at dusk.
I could wow them all by the town square
& I was rich & plump with accolades & hubris.

But now, beloved, I only chew breeze
like khat leaves & suffer daily pesky insults
of fire flies & the florescent African cichlids.

FLAUBERT'S NOTE FOR HIS MARRIED MUSE

Beloved, all noons are not
created equal.
Some are bluer than others
& those are the ones
when your love letters
are not all that comforting & convincing.

On such days please stop by to check on me
& to clench me in your peach-blossom arms
for the longest three minutes

& then rush back to indulge
your jealous husband,
your two demanding toddler-twins,
your half a dozen
Peruvian parakeets which are
as sweet & handsome
as prancing Nicole Miller's models
on walkways in sapphire, amber, amethyst,
olive, teal & plum silks.

GOD'S FOOL

Alberts, they are an old spent couple in their ripe eighties, riper than orange papayas & rose-tinged mangoes. I wonder if God or death savors such over-ripeness? Their pelts are no longer taut as fresh tortillas but never mind we all can't be so blessed to leave in our sleep like an okapi or Pope John Paul The Second. I wonder why God wouldn't even grant us the laity that little lowball of comfort, that little chaser of dignity?

Alberts live in an affluent home built with soft-edged Mexican exterior & swirl of stucco. I love the iterant does in their sprawling backyard garden who drop in every now & then for a quick brunch. I adore those humming birds so taken by bee balms' spiky scarlet-red splendor.

I am a Nicaraguan immigrant.

Alberts ask questions about the vows & sorrows of my country as if their asking can heal my ravaged land. Mrs. Alberts plays scrabble & grins like a nun whenever her arthritis permits her. At times her pain becomes so triumphant that the morphine fizzles out & lets the pain clamp down its tearing claws. I am a day helper—I prepare & serve them lunch & do errands.

Alberts visit doctors often. Mr. Alberts calls the Mrs. my sweet magnolia & brings her flowers—mostly anthuriums & gerbera daisies—with their necks propped up by plastic stems like African necklaces. I reckon their bodies are offering them their respectful farewells & both feel it in their twisting blood, in their jelling bones, in their memories' fuzziness & stalling gestures.

Mr. Alberts' night nurse told me—He has Vascular Fibrosis & given six to eight months to languish. I thought he liked me enough that he could tell me at least that much. But I figure for him dying is a damn embarrassment like wearing diapers. Why tell me—a part-time helper? But they are folks content with their stumbling bridges.

I always wondered about the framed pictures of the handsome boys on the walls of their living room. I ask myself—where are, those sons, in their parents' hour of distress, forlornness & near death.

Today is gilded like my husband's gold-rimmed black velvet Sombrero. I somehow plunked enough spunk to ask Mr. Alberts: "Those boys in the photos-are those your sons? If you don't mind me asking—why they never visit or call or even send flowers?"

I felt as if I had slugged him hard with a tenor sax.

Mr. Alberts with averted doleful glance said after three minutes of swampy silence—"Gabriella. They never call because they were all taken. God summoned them back too soon. Mrs. Alberts and I had four sons. Our first son was stillborn & we just said never mind. We will try again. God can't always be so careful.

We have always been God's fools. Our second son was four when a rare sickness swept him away like a rapid. Our third son when he was seven was run over by an ice-cream van. Our fourth son at age thirty-four went scuba diving in Bermuda's choppy waters & the divers never found his body not even a watch strap to remember him by",

Mr. Alberts said all this without brimming eyes, without a knotted lump in his voice, without a nostalgic twinge, without mulling his hoary blue-finned
catkin-fingers, without hiding his furrowed forehead between his ghostly hands.

I thought these are such valiant souls who don't complain or curse or forswear God; they don't rave or rant or wag their fingers at the perfidious heavens.
At the end what Mr. Alberts said was just this:

"Gabby, It was just our bad luck, Niagras of bad Karma,"

& then he stepped out to take his evening walk. His back glazed with a curled osier of light of some alien order. His creased mane seemed to be going places—
places I would imagine

of *flamingo* radiance.

Palace Of Marvin Gaye

Gonna get it on
Beggin' you, baby, I want to get it on
You don't have to worry that it's wrong
If the spirit moves you, let me groove you good
Let your love come down
Oh, get it on, come on, baby

Do you know I mean it?
I've been sanctified
Hey, hey
Girl, you give me good feelings, so good

Nothin' wrong with love
If you want to love me
Just let yourself go
Oh, baby
Let's get it on

      —Marvin Gaye/Ed Townsend

SWANS IN LOVE

Sharon: my exquisite Isphahan who digs lush samovars & rugs,
my Alhambra of sumptuous arabesque arches & riffs,
my heady amphetamine, my lusty Angel Dust
from whose dreams I wish never to wake up.
You have curtly warned—
You wouldn't make it here till May blossoms,
& until all your classes have shed their hollyhock veils
but that is way too late, my lassi-sipping sitar.
When would I stroke again your zinfandel pomegranates
& bob against the lilac spathe
of your secret water lily?
When will I taste those lips sweeter
than poppy seed kolaches?
My gleaming mother of pearl Florence:
When will I sip your gilded blue bonnet air?
I figure I won't use the pricey Turkish Samovar
& the snazzy china set that I purchased
to match your pink-phlox cheeks, clematis-blue eyes
till I see you lounging on my black leather chaise.

When, beloved, the twin roes of your breasts
could be fed by my kiss-irises.
Let me know if I am hustling you
too much & too often
when I insinuate that I start pining
for your cestrum-red whispers
as soon as you hang-up.
I get aroused lavishly
just thinking of the dianthus evening
when you sipped green tea
with a pinch of raspberry
in my bed in a Botticelli mug
& pretended as if my savvy hands
were not wading against
your bra-less bulbs & you were not growing
minty damp in the underbrush
& losing your fiery animation
in paraphrasing Martin Heidegger.
You started gasping when it was time
to compare him to Carl Jaspers. You just moaned—"I give up!"

At Rachel's birthday party in downtown Madison
cosseted voices swivel & flicker
as undulating electric eels
& silver-black corn snakes.
They vie for my bleary hearing.
The bay window has caught in its passiflora web
a blazing over-wrought moon
sidling through the Ponderosa pines & junipers.
She is showing stress of age & aimless cruising.
I hear a livid wind breaking
the steeds of the poplars & handsome elms.
I think I have sipped too much
of the sunny Puerto Rican rum.
The faded wallpaper flowers in this antechamber
are like peppered moths
draping a lichen-laced Aspen.
A big translucent vase glows
with vermilion lilies, tender freesia eyelids,
orange-eyed calendulas & smoky blue aster stars.

Now, my head is sprinting
with the surge of Johnny Walker
& I dream of you ambling in your Albany home
where for the first time
while your husband groomed
himself in the shower,
ironically singing Paul Simon's
Fifty Ways To Leave Your Lover
we two sipped rosé in the living room
& dared a hushed kiss,
followed by a double fugue,
& then plunged into a triple counterpoint
& then graduated to arpeggio nibbling
till we lost count
& our breaths silvered with mists
& our whispers tinkled
with guilt & delirium.

In Rachel's room a Dali poster
hangs like a sinister queen
on the beige stucco wall
& I burn in your lilac penumbras—
my star-blue-eyed Laila.
Music is menacing
but tempered by warbled phrases.
Gestures are disjointed & insufferable
as if gnawed by a jellyfish.
I hear half muted swearing like furled fists,
bravodic gestures & lush lances of laughter
minced with salted pistachios & crunchy
cucumbers & walnut-spinach salad.
Tonight I met Sadi who is Paul's lover,
Sadi is a gazelle-eyed Iranian senior
worthy of a Rodin or a Michelangelo.

He is in ponytail, a lavender velour shirt,
black denim jeans befitting a satyr.
Paul is fondling his sumptuous rump
like two huge light-pendants—
Paul calls them baklavas.
Over there is Hasan, a Sudanese historian
cum smooth operator
who can't stop ogling & wooing Rachel.
Hasan's pregnant wife is in Khartoum
so he wants to hook up
with any sweet arse femme fatale.
I can't get over how gorgeous Rachel looks
but can't fathom why she has to be
such a super-tease to our lovelorn Hasan.
All this come-hither candle light cleavage
& lips dipped in mint julep
& eyes shot with euphoria
are unbecoming given
that her husband is in Windsor
only eighty miles away lecturing
on "about to become extinct Indian caracal."

Those butterscotch kisses
between the slow-dancing lovers
seem to linger longer on their puckered lips
hotly painted with longing & bourbon
or is it my seething hunger
for your rapacious mouth
that makes the kisses look overlong?
The music is patently Stone Age,
it is shredding & pureeing
every voice register
into an indigo bunting chirping.

My ride tells me that he is
ready to take me home.

Kiss for me your workout-averse
but gorgeous & super-friendly golden retriever,
your fig-blue parakeets
& your laced clarkia-red pillows
nestled against your handsome cheeks.

Whisper my alohas to your raspberry episcia
with metallic pink leaves & ruby blossoms

Yes, I have gallantly memorized all the neat
precincts of your heart!

Post Script:

Enough of those Ella & Armstrong's
phlegmy middle brow standards.

I am relapsing back to
Marvin Gaye's rose windows.

FROLIC

A silk moon like the blossoms
of tall pampas grass demurely trudges
through the creamy
begonia-pink satin lingerie
reminding me of your fussy undressing.

HER FLOWERBED

If you are besotted by those raging fuchsias
cascading down the hanging baskets
or those iris-ballerinas shimmying
in the autumn breeze or if that purple-flecked babushkas
of mustard pansies tug at your epicure heart
& those ocher bacchanals of wild tulips
seem so eager to indulge you
in their bordello of colors & opium
& you just can't get enough of those
crimson schizanthus blossoms
& can't stop gawking
at those African daisies seeding
a silly lump in your throat,
don't feel so guilty or ashamed or "taken".

How could I object or raise an eyebrow
when their bare arse Lolita beauty
mesmerizes me also—I too am a happy prisoner
of their Zen iridescence but when you get tired, mister,
of so much riot of radiance
& need a respite from the garden bugs
nuzzling your face & knees & the heat
has become too rude, too roughneck,
& the bottle of Merlot has basked you
totally in a vermilion delirium
& you feel breezy in your feet
& your lips feel as if ready
to start bonfires please come back in
to lie in my gulmohur arms.
I will summon the gilded ghost
of Marvin Gaye to bless another bower
of heaven for you that I will unbutton
ever so ravishingly for your indulgence!

LUST AS FEATHERED GRASS

At the outset you are raising
an annoying berm of resistance.
It is like driving on a highway
in the direction where a tornado has been
sighted & is imminent
but my up close kisses are inflaming your lips
& are pushing you to a desire-precipice
where fawning is the only balcony.
You are now blistering & buckling
under my caresses hot as feathery grass.
You are now sharing
my lust's high-amped wattage.
You are also flapping under my knees
with your clinched butterfly wings
doubling my pleasure as if you have decided
you will glide along lips-pearl on lips-pearl
breasts locked on breasts & will go wherever
you are escorted till my sails have dropped
the steering winds like burnt up comets.

ENIGMA OF LOVE

Is it to lock your eyes with the beloved
like a knotted pair of gyrating limbs
in a lush tango & feel the mauve rush of Dopamine
in sweet midnight sleeplessness
& to glimpse her lovely face in every lilac bulb,
flute glass of champagne, in the flowing locks of
summer rains & then later in the obsessive spiral
is it to seed beloved's heart with a cloying guilt
by warning her—"if you ever leave me,

I will trapeze down San Fran's scarlet bridge
or jump off from Sears' Tower" or is to sense
in your sly guts that you could do no better
so you are better off staying with the current lover
or is to cuddle her with vriesea-red adorations
& lavish her with dinners in jazz-clubs & Ritz-Carlton
till a fresher & cuter one appears & promenade
into your sense-atrium & pulls you in her iris-arms
& not let you leave at least for a few months?

THE LUCKY PAUSE

I tell you—I want to kiss your intimate analgesic
castanets, triangles, cymbals, the cello suppleness
& all the lilac gorges. You smile back
like a sweet bodhisattva knowing
where all this pleading will end up.
You protest that you have to get the beef roast going
for your teenage daughter due in an hour.
And then after some heavy duty solicitation
you consent to a fifteen minutes long rapture.
We slink in your squeaky, queen size bed
that your ex has left as a gesture of amity & kindness.
My hands are perched on your jasmine hips.
You are already quivering like the
monsoon-roused palms in Florida Springs.
We are tasting the thump of our hearts
on our suckled tongues.
Your hand grabbing my revved up sex
to make it sing its clanking aria.
We are two twined horses with blazing nostrils,
two playful over-zealous inebriated lion-cubs
clawing, pinning & baiting each other,
two tangoing cobras spit-firing
into raspy, knotted, pivoted genitals.

Your nettled sex swivels & flounces
to ply the thrusts of my steaming piston.
Your eyes are closed buds in a fast flooding of silver mines.
I am an electric eel wading into your coral reefs.
We are now seesawing together, perspiring like lumberjacks
till nature lets go its last jitters & wind leaves the festooned sails.
We are now lying on the sheets, slack-limbed, almost famished
& quite eager to back paddle to our deferred orbits
to become the busy photons again
to dance our solo quantum ballet.
We put on our headgear, check our silencers,
our visors, our nagging beepers, our riggings.
Our parting kisses are too civil too ceremonious,
our caresses too tempered, too pash-slaked.
We are now two gleaming Harleys to stagger the highways,
two sweaty narcissuses leaving for x, y axes.

THE KISS

She was no Venus of Urbino by Titian
neither was she a sultry Playboy centerfold
from U of Kentucky or a vixen Chanel model
in frilly pink silks
cascading down from a spiral staircase.
Nor she was a Valentino epiphany
in lilac crepe short dress
& mauve satin skirt striding a catwalk.
She didn't even have a glittering
karat gold ruby ring from Tiffany

but when he would press his lips
against her lychee mouth
& she would close her violet
dew flower eyelids
like butterfly wings,
he knew he was gulping paradise.

IN THE KEY OF RAPTURE

René, my good mate from Prague,
I notice that you often consorted
with half a dozen riveting muses
like scarlet ibises blazing over
white-golden cotton fields
& you penned sheaves of ruby-flecked
elegies & sonnets as inebriating
as martinis with strawberry nectar
& raspberry vodka but I
without those enchanting cheerleaders
didn't fare too far behind.
Just imagine, dear comrade poet,
if I could only have a quarter
of your leisure & some of your great luck
in radiant groupies how much deeper
& often I could have dipped & plunged
in the key of rapture,
how many more hyacinth-macaw poems
would have nestled this rainbow heart.

JUST AN ORDINARY BARD

I am no funk soldier, whale caller or whale rider
with a kelp horn or a John Coltrane protégé
hell bent on setting Carnegie Hall ablaze.
I am neither a chaser of tornados' skirts
or a horse breaker or a horse whisperer
nor a trapper of rivers, founder of cities,
trainer of raging melanomas or wily lions.
I am just an ordinary bard with a lavish pen
learning to love your fritillaria pheromones,
odalisque palette of your moods so that
you may love me back.

A FLAUBERTIAN RIFF

Who can match, blossom for blossom,
the blue-poppy promenades of my lines,
make love to a gorgeous call girl
from the Andalusian Quarter
in a three-star Paris motel
& later treat her richly like a princess
in an Indonesian bistro with sizzling
Sambel Urang shrimps & luxuriously
chili-sauced chicken livered
Rempelo-ati & still be welcomed
in his Lord God's forgiving arms?

YOUR KISSES

Who knows, beloved, if I have ever written
a timeless stanza or a canto worthy to be cited
by a school girl in her English finals
but this much I know for certain
like the sure caress of a thundering sun
that your kisses in this gathering dusk
are sepals of eternal & will kindle my heart
till I am delivered to a pearl-blue angel.

How Many Ways!

From her poppy white Honda sedan
my swiveling genet walks her dominatrix walk
out-dancing my heart.

She is a sensuous Ellington tune.
She is a Heifetz serenade in bloom.
She is my Berber gift from the rolling green hills
of Morocco. Her dad was a horseman
& she rode barebacked horses in her early teens,
she is my blue Methadone dream,
she is my sister in sin.
She is my gorgeous prayer mat.

What fabled California wines can you think of
one must hoard to bathe her jasmine bulbs?
Her smile ignites her Sassanian pearl teeth,
her giggles' neons are a war chest of diamonds.
Decked in fresh tan, gold-dappled sunglasses,
she pouts her lips painted with coral bells
lipstick & a hint of Burgundy,
She is draped in hot flora of Armani's fantasy:
the sheer blue top, the black silk pants with slits
& blue velvet bolero jacket.

She is well schooled in hip-hop & Hafiz,
she purrs with perfume of *Poême*.
In how many argots & dialects, polyglot God
of Mallarmé & Octavio Paz,
should I count my blessings?
How many billboards of ballads
to paint my thankfulness?
How many *Kama Sutra* & Tantric angles
to sow a rapture's babushka?

Lord God of Warren Beatty & Madonna,
how many ways should I deluge the honeycombs
of my young lynx to make you think
I am grateful & honored
& to make her come back
for sumptuous seconds & thirds!

SIX RUBAIYAT FOR BELOVED'S BRACELET

1

Beloved, we lived our lives as if
death was a vapid overblown rumor
& when it entered our violet boudoir
we just faked it was an uncanny rapture.

2

Love, God, friendships—We now surmise
are all star-tasseled glamorous lies
but like the soaring birds of paradise
only great cantos rise towards the skies.

3

I wonder what is the greater fret & menace
that is plaguing this gasping tanager heart—
the anguish of never publishing my work
or being discovered—I was a phony bard.

4

Your kisses inflamed my lips & loins,
that day the sky was an Egyptian belly dancer
but the noon you left me for a failed actor
the day had morphed into a Madrid massacre.

5

Those eyes were lagoons in which
I saw black swans & water lilies.
Those cheeks won over red ginger
blossoms & buds of Gerber daisies.

6

Don't call me a sell-out when you already conceded
if I had exceeded the safe & sound Rilkean rhymes
even *you* my love would have declined to scamper
with me over my poems' treacherous landmines.

Pietà

So what if their smoke-light sluggish
responses were soaked in jealousy's toxins

& their eyes flared with racial slurs
& pitted contempt.

That they all blocked our entrance
to Glory's driveway like mafia thugs
& Blackshirts.

That they made it quite certain
our flames wouldn't outlive
our last whimpers

that there would be no rebirths,
no revivals,
no resurrections.

We must still be grateful, dear heart,
that they couldn't stop
our poems' hurricanes,

that the poems came
like a tempest of miracles,

budded asters in their
rosy florescence.

That despite their shrill censures
we had such marvelous rollicking fun
dolling up the English language

& so many hearty laughs
at God's expense.

Remember, there are only few of us
lucky enough who could even say that much
at their sojourn's end.

About the Author

Yousuf Zaigham was born in Lucknow, India. His poems have appeared in *Afkar*, *Fonoon* & *Seep*, leading literary journals in Urdu. *Like A Vermeer and Other Poems* is his first poetry collection in English. His exuberant poems traverse the bridge between Eastern & Western poetic canons. He resides in Colorado with his wife and two cats.

978-0-595-40974-
0-595-40974-1

Printed in the United States
65251LVS00006B/38